Dream Decoder

Dream Decoder

INTERPRET OVER 1,000 DREAM SYMBOLS

Joules Taylor

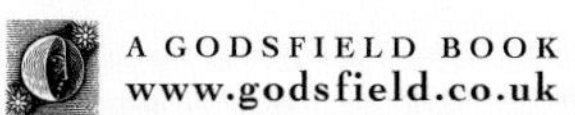

With thanks
to Ken – for taking over while I dream,
to Kai – for sharing your dreams with me,
to Amanda – whose dreams are almost as interesting as my own,
and to my own subconscious, for many, many years of fun, fear and fascination.

First published in Great Britain in 2006 by
Godsfield Press, a division of Octopus Publishing Group Ltd
2-4 Heron Quays, London E14 4JP

ISBN-13: 978-1-84181-307-3
ISBN-10: 1-84181-307-9

A CIP catalogue record for this book is available from the British Library

Printed and bound in China
Designed by Grade Design Ltd, London

10 9 8 7 6 5 4 3 2 1

Contents

INTRODUCTION

Dreaming. It's something we all do – something we have to do to retain our mental and emotional health – yet despite centuries of study, dreams remain a mystery. We may know the mechanism of dreaming, the firing of synapses in the brain, but our dreams themselves are an intricate, intimate mix of memory, wishes, fears and desires, an evolving code we write within ourselves every time we fall asleep. They offer a deeply personal insight into our own minds, our own subconscious. Learning to decode our dreams provides a key to understanding ourselves.

WHAT ARE DREAMS?

The importance of dreaming is clear from its prominence in all cultures and throughout time, from the Aboriginal Dreamtime and ancient Greece and Egypt, where dreams were seen as messages from the gods, through Freud's and Jung's psychoanalytical theories, to the current thinking that dreams are a way of 'rebooting' the brain, getting rid of any mental clutter and internal conflicts while we sleep. But where do the actual images come from? What do they mean? Most of all, what can they teach us?

Dream dictionaries have existed since around 2000 BCE, where they were found in Middle Kingdom Egypt, and are still being written and used today. However, they have one drawback: they are usually either based on older, outdated works or are, essentially, lists of **somebody else's** meanings for the symbols, people, places and objects that appear in dreams. Such interpretations might apply to a few people other than the author, but the only way to understand our own dreams is to establish the meanings for ourselves.

This book is designed to enable us to interpret our **own** dreams, devise our own personal 'dream thesaurus', learn how our own minds work, and in doing so gain a richer experience of life **throughout** our life; dream meanings can change over time as we grow and develop.

The individual interpretations in this book detail some of the basic meanings of the symbols and situations in dreams, drawn from a wide variety of sources including psychology, myth and global archetypes, but leave plenty of room for you to analyse and note your own meanings.

THE SCIENCE OF SLEEP AND DREAMING

Sleep and dreaming happen in cycles consisting of five stages.

1 The hypnagogic state, where the body relaxes and prepares for sleep. This stage is characterized by a sensation of floating or drifting often accompanied by a jumble of voices and images of vague landscapes or shifting colours.

2 The initial stage. The eyes are closed, the brain is still awake, but moving towards sleep, and generating alpha waves, which can enhance creativity and inspiration.

3 True sleep. The brain is now generating theta brainwaves.

4 Deep sleep, characterized by delta brainwaves. At this stage waking is very difficult, and often accompanied by an almost irresistible need to go back to sleep.

5 Dreaming. Characterized by Rapid Eye Movement (REM), this stage lasts about ten minutes initially, increasing to about an hour towards the end of the night's sleep.

After stage five, the brain returns to stage two and the cycle starts over again. Each cycle lasts around 90 minutes, so in an eight-hour night's sleep the average person will have at least four dreams and possibly many more.

During dreaming the body experiences a temporary paralysis in which we can only move fingers and toes, eyes and face. This is a safety measure to stop us acting out our more dangerous dreams – flying, running, climbing – in our sleep. Sleepwalking happens when the paralysis is incomplete or fails to operate.

The memory of our dreams is often vivid on waking, but fades rapidly unless we take definite steps to record our memories.

Dreaming is vital for our health. Without it, we become stressed, anxious, irritable and unable to concentrate; our blood pressure rises, we may feel dizzy and sweat more than necessary. Prolonged periods without dreaming may result in difficulty in learning, and the stress on the body could be dangerous.

Make time to dream. At the very least, ensure that you sleep for a minimum of three hours at a time, allowing yourself two dream cycles.

Precognitive dreams

Precognitive dreams are those which foretell the future, usually disasters, both natural and man-made. Given that there are billions of people in the world, all of them dreaming at some point, and that many of them will dream of disasters of some sort or another, it's understandable that most of these 'precognitive' dreams will simply be coincidences – even if they **have** saved lives by stopping people getting into a car, train or plane that later crashed. However, there is some evidence that such dreams do happen – they are notable for being extremely specific.

While I was at university I dreamed that the father of a fellow student had died suddenly, and the student was devastated and weeping. I woke up with a start and looked at the clock: it was around 2.30 a.m. I had never met the man, nor dreamed of him before or since, and he was, as far as anyone knew, in good health. I was friendly with but not particularly close to the daughter. The following mid-morning I met the student, who was in tears and surrounded by friends. Her father had died at the same time as the dream, but she hadn't found out until breakfast time when a counsellor had visited to break the news.

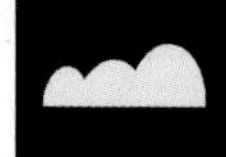

Lucid dreams

Lucid dreams are those in which the dreamer is aware of dreaming and may be able to take control, directing the dream in the direction they wish it to progress.

Such dreams are rare – but there are steps you can take that might help you to learn how to dream lucidly. Once you're in the habit of recording your dreams (see page 14) and are finding it easier to remember the details, try writing 'Tonight I will have a lucid dream' on a piece of paper before you go to sleep. It's surprising how often the brain will obey a written command!

You could also instruct yourself about the subject of your dream. Keep the instruction simple to start with – suggest you go swimming, or flying, do something you enjoy in dreams. If that works, later you can try giving yourself more complicated commands.

Don't be discouraged if it doesn't work. Even people who practise lucid dreaming only succeed about 25 per cent of the time. And even if you never achieve conscious control the effort is worthwhile, as you may succeed in influencing your dreams, for example changing a nightmare into something much more pleasant.

Surreal dreams

Some dreams are simple and easy to understand. Others are more complex, with a variety of images and events, and it may take some time to examine and interpret each element and how they fit together. Some may be wholly influenced by something that has happened recently in your waking life – a play, film or book that deeply affected you, for example, or an important work project that's preying on your mind. The most difficult to interpret, however, are surreal dreams.

Surreal dreams have their own internal logic, which usually bears little or no relation to waking world logic. Here's an example:

'I was floating outside what looked like a clear plastic cube with a three-dimensional maze inside. Everything was bathed in a beautiful blue light. At a top corner of the maze was a tall, long-haired elf; in the opposite, bottom corner a dark shadowy figure I couldn't properly make out. They both had to make their way to the centre of the cube, but only the first to arrive could escape. They also had to try to kill each other on the way. To complicate matters further, after a steadily decreasing cycle of time the maze shifted through

both time and space, with floor becoming ceiling and vice versa, or turning inside out. It was also shrinking, making it more and more difficult for the two inside to move. I was interested but strangely impassive. I woke before I found out who won, but this didn't bother me in the least.'

Despite the surreal and attractive trappings, the dream essentially expresses the common theme of light (the mythical elf) and dark (the shadow) vying for dominance in a maze, which here most likely represents the dreamer's mind. The fact that the dreamer was outside simply observing, unconcerned as to who won, suggests he or she feels detached from the struggle, possibly superior to it. The fact that the setting kept changing and becoming more dangerous suggests an awareness of time running out for the struggle.

When considering a dream of this type, pare away the lightshow and look at the basics!

Nightmares

Nightmares usually start off as ordinary dreams, turning unpleasant as they progress. The worst thing about nightmares is the feeling of helplessness they engender. They are usually a reflection of how you feel about occurrences or fears in your waking life – and any given dream has the potential to turn into a nightmare. Occasionally a nightmare will be your subconscious 'punishing' you, pointing out that perhaps you feel you need punishing for something you have or haven't done.

There are effectively three points of view in a nightmare, implying three different fears: the action is happening to you; you are watching it happen to someone else, often someone very close; or you yourself are performing the action against someone else. This last is the rarest of the three and is often indicative of strong negative feelings you hold against the individual in question.

RECORDING YOUR DREAMS – THE DREAM DIARY

The equipment you need is simple:

- a notebook or journal and pen to keep beside the bed, to record dreams on waking. Keep it only for this purpose and choose one you enjoy using
- another notebook (or computer file) for listing personal interpretations of dream symbols and situations
- this book for reference
- the willingness to dedicate a small amount of time and thought to the process.

Getting into the habit of recording your dreams is probably the most difficult part of the process, especially if your mornings are usually busy, but it is possible, and becomes easier with time as you train your brain to remember. On occasions when you simply don't have the time to write anything, at the very least lie still for a couple of minutes before you rise, running the dream through your mind as though you were watching a film. Make time to record it later in as much detail as possible.

Note everything you remember, no matter how vague; make sketches if it helps. Try to recall feelings and atmosphere as well as images. If nothing else, record what went through your mind on waking. You **will** eventually be able to remember – it simply takes practice.

Once the dream has been recorded, it can be interpreted – and that's where the enjoyment begins. There are several questions you need to ask yourself, repeatedly, when examining your dreams.

- What was the mood of the dream?
- Did anything happen recently to spark this dream – watching a stirring or memorable film before retiring, or an argument with someone, for example?

- Could the dream have been caused or influenced by external things – a car alarm, for example, or being too hot or cold?
- Is it a recurring dream – one you have more than once – or does it contain recurring images?
- What do the symbols mean to you personally?

Remember that the mind often uses visual puns and word-plays to express itself, and may draw on cultural sayings and proverbs to illustrate its dream meanings.

The interpretations can be surprising, and are always revealing. Exploring our minds is an exhilarating, enlightening and immensely satisfying practice – and a better understanding of ourselves can lead to greater self-confidence, self-reliance, self-fulfilment, and an increased ability to deal successfully with life.

INTERPRETING THE DREAMSCAPE

Our dreams happen in our own personal dreamscape: it can be a fascinating and occasionally frightening place. Sometimes we'll find ourselves somewhere that bears little or no resemblance to anywhere we've been in the waking world, yet we'll know immediately where we are. It's our inner world, where almost anything can happen. It's even possible to draw a map of such places, and over time we can get to know our dreamscape intimately.

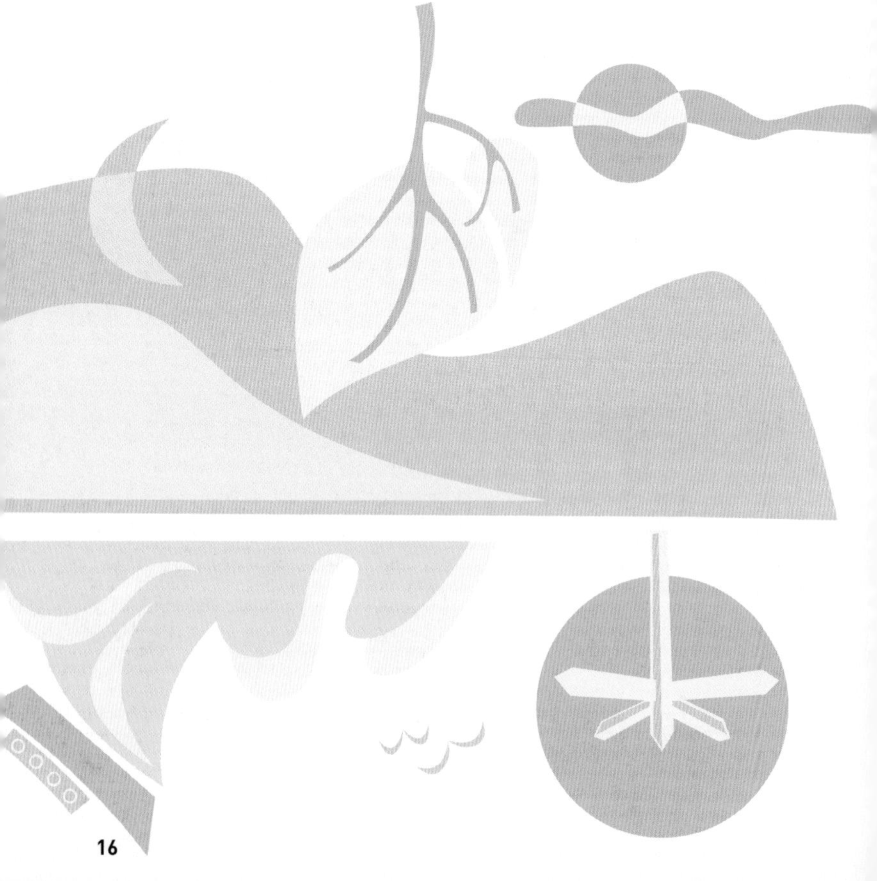

Once you have the dream recorded, consider the circumstances. Was the place familiar? Were you alone? If not, who was with you? Were there any animals in sight? What was the weather like? What time of day was it? What did you do? Perhaps most importantly, how did you feel – did you enjoy the dream?

If you find yourself returning to a particular location in your dreams, especially if it's one you don't recognize from waking life, pay it special attention: it's obviously significant to you. Does it symbolize a refuge from the world? Perhaps a source of inspiration or creativity? If it's a dark, unpleasant place, does it represent a lurking fear, something or someone in your daily life you perceive as a subtle threat?

It often happens that a series of locations or events run together in dreams; sometimes it may be difficult to decide whether you have had one dream or several. The best way to untangle them is to interpret all the elements and see if they fall naturally into separate segments. Occasionally you'll find the dream was episodic, with each segment following on from the previous one. Such dreams may provide guidance to an ongoing waking life event or situation.

Remember that dreams reveal our inner selves, and the fact that we may not like what we find out does not make it any less real or valid. Everyone has their dark side. Understanding it is the first step to acceptance, and from there we can work towards integration, tolerance and the achievement of lasting well-being.

USING THIS BOOK

This book provides over 1,000 symbols and themes that can occur in dreams, arranged in thematic groups within the following chapters. These range from clearly defined images such as people you know, animals or recognizable landscapes to more ephemeral elements such as colour, space or time (such as a sense of it being morning) or a feeling of hopelessness or joy.

Plenty of cross-references are included to lead you from one aspect of an image to another (such as Pilot to Flying), but you may also find the comprehensive index a most useful guide, especially until you are familiar with where to find specific images and topics.

Each entry has a brief description of the image and, where applicable, how it may appear in a dream and some background information on its symbolism or history. This is followed by some questions and notes to ask yourself, to help you interpret what that element of the dream might mean for you. One person's tranquil, re-energizing solitary walk along a beach, for example, may be another's vision of terrifying loneliness. Never forget that dreams are reflections of our own minds, so what it means to you will reflect your waking life, your past experience and your subconscious.

Few dreams involve only one image, so read about all the elements you have noted from your dream and consider how they interact and what they might mean together. At first, your conclusions may be disjointed or uncertain, but your interpretation skills will improve with practice.

Happy dreaming!

1 THE NATURAL WORLD

From landscapes and weather to minerals, stones, plants and animals, symbols from nature can provide extremely powerful and significant dream images. As with all dreams, consider what the image means to you. For example, do bulrushes remind you of the biblical story of Moses, or make you think of calm summer days by the river?

PLACES

Forest

In dreams, forests often represent our shared past, when we lived by hunting and gathering. They symbolize a way of life that's simpler than today in many respects, though more physically demanding, and with different dangers.

In your dream: Were you walking, relaxing and enjoying the wonderful sense of peace and serenity that forests provide? Perhaps your subconscious is yearning for a more active way of life, or a spell away from its trials. Were you **hunting** to feed yourself or to prove your skills? Or were you **lost**, and if so, do you feel lost in your waking life, overwhelmed by your surroundings? Were you hiding from someone, or trying to escape from some sort of danger? Or were you trying to protect the forest from logging or pollution, for example? What animals were you aware of? Were you with others or alone – and how did you feel?
(See also Wild Animals, pages 80–89; Woodsman, page 174; Hunter, page 190)

Wood

Woods are forests' younger siblings. They're smaller, generally less ancient and less awe-inspiring. It's easier to feel at home in a wood than in a forest. Dreams of walking or sheltering in a wood are usually beneficial, suggesting strong inner resources and a positive mental attitude.

In your dream: Was the wood healthy and alive or dead or dying? If it was the latter it might be wise to consider if there's an element of your life you're neglecting or denying.
(See also Trees, pages 49–56)

Crossroads

Whether paved, tarmac or a natural place where two forest trails cross, dreaming of a crossroads means you have come to a crossroads in your life and must choose which path to take. There is usually some sort of indicator to point out the options, though it might not be as straightforward as a signpost. Your choice might be between an easy option that will take you nowhere as regards your career, or a much harder course that will result in promotion and more responsibility, and possibly a larger salary. The decision is likely to affect your future for some considerable time, so considering the dream carefully is advisable.

In your dream: Is the path before you wide, flat and easy or dark, overgrown and torturous? Is there someone or something to point you along the right path, possibly an animal or someone you trust?

Jungle

Jungles are wild, often dangerous places, ancient and primitive but with an immense appeal. Dreaming of being in a jungle suggests a desire or need to make contact with your instincts, your wilder self, the darker, hidden side of your psyche. If the dream was enjoyable, it indicates that you are comfortable with that aspect of yourself: finding the jungle a frightening place suggests the opposite, that you are afraid or ashamed of your darker nature.

In your dream: Were you alone, or was someone with you – and if so, who? Were you happy for them to see your dark side, or embarrassed that they were there? If the latter, your mind might be suggesting that you know the person couldn't cope with understanding you properly, and therefore a deep relationship may be out of the question.
(See also Animals, pages 74–110)

Plain

Wide open spaces covered with grasses and low shrubs, plains have an almost romantic appeal. Unlike forests (see page 20), where it's difficult to see for any distance ahead, on a plain the panorama is broad, the horizon far distant.

In your dream: Were you being hunted, or walking towards a specific goal? The plain is quite a threatening place – you are exposed and can be seen easily. Do you feel exposed in your waking life? As though someone or something might be stalking you? Is it a familiar threat, or a vague feeling of dread? If it's a frequent dream, consider what's causing it.
(See also Running to Escape, page 144)

Mountain

Mountains generally represent both ambitions and the obstacles hindering their attainment, and unless you live near or climb them regularly, their significance in dreams is usually fairly straightforward. The higher the mountain, the bigger the ambitions; the ease or otherwise of the climb reflects your perception of how easy it will be to realize them. Standing at the top of a mountain, gazing out at the view below suggests you feel you have realized or almost realized your ambition. If you don't feel exultant or joyful, you might like to take a closer look at your desires and dreams. It may be that they aren't really yours; they might be a parent's or lover's ambitions for you, for example, and realizing them feels like a hollow victory.

In your dream: Were you being carried up a mountain? This suggests you anticipate others smoothing the way for you, possibly even doing much of the necessary work. If you are carrying someone, it indicates that you feel you are doing this in some form in your waking life.
(See also Climbing, page 216)

Hill

The symbolism is similar to that for mountain, but the ambitions are much more modest and most often more easily attainable. The view from the top may not be as spectacular as from a mountain, but it is no less appealing for all that.

In your dream: If your hill is a slag-heap are you trying to live up to someone else's vision of you?
(See also Climbing, page 216)

Desert

Deserts can be energizing or terrifying depending on the circumstances and your personal feelings.

In your dream: Were you lost or abandoned, with no water or protection from the sun? Do you feel 'deserted' in waking life, left alone in an arid environment to shrivel in the heat? Does your life resemble a desert at the moment, empty, dry and barren? Or was the desert a challenge, a way for you to prove yourself strong and capable by escaping unscathed? If so, how did you make your way back to civilization? Did you have help and, if so, from whom or what?

If you found the dream desert beautiful, a lonely but tranquil place, it may be that you need to escape from the hectic pace of waking life for a while, to recoup your energy in peace and as far away from other people as you can go.

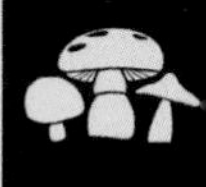

Moor

Moorland rises from the surrounding countryside, broad, expansive and open to all weathers. It's associated with solitude and serenity, being above the hurly-burly of town and city, a wild and lonely place.

Walking on a moor in dreams suggests a yearning for solitude, some time for yourself, unless you're heading for a specific location, in which case the moor most likely represents the effort needed to achieve your goal.

In your dream: Do you see the journey as a necessary evil? In which case, are you moving with determination, oblivious to the landscape around you? Your subconscious might be suggesting you take a little time to appreciate the view along the way – enjoy the journey as well as the reaching of your objective, expand your mind instead of focusing solely on the job at hand.

Gorge

Gorges are clefts in the earth, caused by weather or ground movement over millennia. From a small fissure to something on the scale of the Grand Canyon, gorges in dreams can represent either a major obstacle to be overcome – the ground opening up under your feet – or a clever, if perilous way through a problem.

In your dream: What did you do? Back away from the gorge, try to go around it, cross it via a bridge, or climb down in order to climb up the other side? Or were you able to fly or jump across it? Each suggests either the way you approach problems in your waking life – or perhaps a method you subconsciously think might be more successful, prompting you to see your problems in a different light.

River

Life has been likened to a river, with its bends, deeps and shallows, and its continually changing landscape. In dreams, the river symbolizes life's journey, from birth to death and beyond.

A river dream can be a significant indicator of how you feel about the way your life is going. A dream of **struggling in the middle of a river**, unable to reach either bank and being swept away, is a fairly straightforward symbol of loss of control, as is being **stuck in a backwater** or a tangle of weeds, unable to make any progress.

Dreaming of a number of small rivers may indicate several different life paths you could take.

In your dream: Are you sitting beside the river, watching life go by? Are you resting for a while, or are you stuck there, out of the flow? Are you walking alongside it, moving at a slower pace to get your breath back? Are you moving upstream, against the flow, trying to get back to an earlier time of your life, or going with the flow, making the best of any opportunities that present themselves?
(See also Bridge, page 323)

Stream

Streams are small rivers. They may become larger as they continue on their way, or they may end in a pool or lake, or even dive underground. Dreaming specifically of a stream may symbolize a certain period in your life when you need to step away from the mainstream of life for a while, to reflect on where your life is going.

In your dream: If the stream flows along a gorge (see page 25) are you being forced in one particular direction, even if it's not your desired path? Is the stream full of large boulders, making its course noisy and tumultuous? Perhaps you see your waking life as stony, full of irritations, if not outright problems. Can you see a way out?

Lake

Lakes epitomize the saying 'still waters run deep': they usually symbolize profound emotion, the feelings most often kept hidden rather than those on the surface.

Feeling happy, peaceful and comfortable in the dream indicates that you're happy with yourself and your emotional life. Feeling afraid, or uneasy, suggests that you aren't comfortable with your emotions, perhaps perceiving yourself as vulnerable when you let others see how you really feel.

In your dream: Does the lake represent you, or someone else? Were you beside it, or actually sailing on or swimming in it? Were you exploring around the edge, or venturing out of your depth?

Dreaming of a monster in a lake strongly suggests a fear of the power of your hidden emotions, and of losing control of them. Are you being too rigidly self-controlled?
(See also Swimming, page 213; Monster, page 376)

Pool

Natural pools are, in effect, lakes on a smaller scale, and the same symbolism applies.

In your dream: Was the pool magical in some way, perhaps possessing an elemental creature. Or was it to be used for a specific purpose, as a source of fish for food, for example, or for bathing? These suggest that you rely on your feelings for emotional sustenance, or to keep you cleansed of the unpleasantness of the modern world, and are positive symbols.
(See also Fisherman, page 174; Fish, page 108)

Waterfall

From gentle tropical cascades to Niagara Falls, waterfalls are beautiful, impressive features. The endless tumbling water and the sound can be mesmerizing, drawing the eye and the mind down to the spray – or ripples – in the pool or river. It has been suggested, also, that waterfalls in dreams symbolize the memory of being born, but only you can decide whether that meaning applies to you!

In your dream: What was the emotion associated with the waterfall? Awe? Contentment? Release? Were you bathing in the waterfall or just looking at it? A dream of bathing under the cascade may suggest a desire to be 'washed clean' of the problems of your waking life, if you enjoyed the experience. Alternatively, especially if the dream was accompanied by feelings of dread, do you feel that life is battering you, trying to 'wash you away'? Can you swim? If not, it might be a good idea to try to find a way out of your current difficulties.
(See also Swimming, page 213)

Sea

The sea in dreams typically represents both the warm ancient oceans from which we all originally came, and the depths of our subconscious minds. Swimming in a rough sea and enjoying it indicates you enjoy challenge; not enjoying swimming, whether the sea is rough or smooth, suggests insecurity, some difficulty in dealing with the fundamentals of life, especially your emotions.

Swimming under the water suggests the ability or desire to explore yourself, your mind and motivations, and is an encouraging, positive image. **Paddling** or wading may indicate a certain reluctance to engaging fully with life, a tendency to stand to one side and observe rather than wading in and participating.

In your dream: What was the weather like and state of the water – smooth and tranquil or agitated, even rough? What was the surrounding landscape – bay or beach (see page 30), cliffs or seaside town, familiar or somewhere strange. Were you on holiday, on a quick visit or did you live there? What feelings were associated with the scene? (See also Swimming, page 213; Water, page 63)

Seashore, beach

A broad, **sandy beach** suggests a broad mind, unless you were floundering through deep fine sand, indicating a fear of time passing while you are going nowhere. A **stony or rocky beach**, painful to walk on, suggests that you find the concerns of your waking life difficult: alternatively, it may indicate you're simply going through a difficult patch at the moment – especially if you can see more comfortable ground ahead.

Rough sea to one side and a steep cliff on the other, with you between them, symbolizes being caught 'between the devil and the deep blue sea', forced to make a difficult choice as to the lesser of two evils.

In your dream: What was the beach like? What were you doing there – holidaying, working, or on a journey? Most importantly, what were your feelings?

Cliff

Cliffs are dangerous places and should be treated with respect – rockfalls and landslides can happen without warning.

In your dream: Are you 'standing on the edge of a cliff' in your waking life, about to take an irrevocable step that will probably end in disaster – such as making permanent a relationship that your subconscious knows is going to result in misery for you? Successfully climbing the cliff suggests that you know instinctively which is the best choice.
(See also Climbing, page 216)

Icescape

The Arctic and Antarctic are places of extremes, too cold for humans to survive without very specialized equipment. Mostly devoid of plant growth, they are nevertheless places of brutal, overwhelming beauty. Dreaming of being alone in such a landscape is a symbol of inner solitude and emotional detachment.

In your dream: Were you there willingly? In which case, do you need to 'cool off' emotionally or mentally, get some distance from a person or situation that is really making you angry? If unwillingly, do you feel that you've been abandoned, left to fend for yourself in a hostile environment?

Alternatively, you may be facing an immense challenge in your waking life, and the only way to succeed will be to 'keep a cool head'. Are the people you're involved with helpful, or holding you back?

Cave

A cave most often represents the womb, a mysterious place hidden from the outside world – though wombs are usually a lot warmer than most caves. There can be sexual metaphor here if the cave is reached via a tunnel, symbolizing the vagina, entrance to the womb.

In your waking life: Do you feel safe and secure? Or claustrophobic and panicky? Is your mother-figure supportive or using emotional blackmail to keep you close? Alternatively, are you trying to regain the security of the womb and have someone else take charge for a while? The dream may be warning you to de-stress before you literally end up with someone having to care for you – in hospital, for example. (See also Mother, page 136)

COUNTRIES AND CONTINENTS

Dreaming of an identifiable region often indicates your unconscious feelings towards a nation and its people – countries are multi-layered entities, with different characters. A dream of a specific state or city may be complex and reflect a wish, desire or fear, depending on the flavour of the dream, whether you've visited it in person, and how you feel about it in waking life.

Africa

The 'Dark Continent', traditionally mysterious, romantic, lush and fertile – a volatile place, sometimes violent, but brimful of life in all its richness and variety.

In your dream: What was the setting, and what does it tell you about yourself? A Bedouin tent in the desert, harking back to ancient traditions and a simpler way of life? The excitement of a safari, interacting with potentially dangerous wild animals? Sharing the life of a tribal people, learning their secrets of survival? Exploring the sights and sounds of a modern African city? Or delving into the past, investigating the pyramids or the Sphinx?

American Continent

From the chill northern coasts of Canada to the storms of Cape Horn, the hectic pace of New York to laid-back, sunny California, the majestic grandeur of the Andes mountains to the lush vitality of the Amazon rain forest, this vast continent encompasses nearly every terrain and culture on the planet.

In your dream: Were you on holiday, enjoying the sights and sounds of an exciting new experience, or working, taking advantage of the opportunities offered? Where exactly were you, and what does that place mean to you in waking life? What message did the dream hold for you?

Asia

From the highest mountains on earth to the ultra-modern cities of Japan, Asia is exotic, complex, vibrant and dynamic. It encompasses the brilliant colour, movement and magnificent architecture of India, the extraordinary beauty of Thailand, the ancient mystical serenity of China. It also encompasses abject poverty, inequality, the destructive nature of extreme weather, and drugs.

In your dream: Why were you there? To learn, sitting at the feet of a guru? To explore the ancient civilizations? To broaden your mind and understanding? If you were there unwillingly, was it to teach you some kind of a lesson, about charity, tolerance or perseverance, perhaps?
(See also Japanese Maple, page 52)

Australia

The country symbolizes a dichotomy between the very ancient and the very modern, between the Aboriginal Dreamtime and the bustling modern cities.

In your dream: Australia suggests a wish for wide open spaces and warmth, a love of the unusual and quirky, and a longing for perceived frankness and openness.

Middle East

Tradition-bound, fiercely autonomous and frequently conflict-ridden, these hot and dry countries are the birthplace of the main patriarchal religions. A dream of visiting the area can be complex: try to note any other accompanying symbols. A weapon, for example, could suggest you can be militant where your faith is concerned.

In your dream: Why were you there? Were you fighting, or on holiday? Exploring or reaffirming your faith? Who was with you? What did you do? What did you learn?
(See also Desert, page 24)

Europe

What does Europe mean to you? Bureaucracy or a vast reservoir of learning, history, artistic and literary wealth? A chaotic mix of languages and cultures jostling each other? The cradle of civilization? Places you wish to visit, or avoid?

In your dream: It's likely that your mind perceives individual countries in the often unfortunate stereotypes they've acquired down the ages: fiery and flamboyant Spain, laid-back and lascivious Italy, staid and phlegmatic England. Which country was in the dream, and which aspects of it were most apparent? What were you feeling? Are they aspects of your own character you like or loathe? Or were you simply enjoying experiencing something different?

Russia

Russia has seen more than its fair share of strife and unrest, yet it remains associated with old power and majesty. Ask yourself what Russia conjures up for you in waking life. Dr Zhivago or the Cold War, oppressive regime or colourful history?

In your dream: What were you doing? Enjoying the sophistication of the cities, or appalled by the poverty and destitution of parts of the country? Riding through it in luxury, or trekking across its steppes? Russia has often been linked to spy-films: were you on some sort of secret mission? How does this relate to your normal life – wish-fulfilment or fear of 'reds under the bed'?
(See also Icescape, page 31; Spy, page 177)

SPACE

Sun

The sun usually represents the heart, the centre of either the dreamer or the person closest to them: it can also symbolize warmth, stability, safety, summer and abundance.

Sunrise in dreams symbolizes beginnings – the start of a new day with all its potential, the start of a new relationship, job or phase of life. **Midday** represents work in progress, while **sunset**, especially a beautiful sunset, symbolizes endings, satisfaction with a job well done or a life well spent.

In your waking life: What stage of life have you reached? Do you feel it's a time of new beginnings or have you achieved what you set out to do? What are your relationships with the significant people in your life? The sun has been perceived as being female in the past, symbolizing the mother who feeds and protects her children, and may represent your primary care-giver or the most important person in your life, whether male or female.

Moon

The moon symbolizes complexity and mystery, change, the passage of time and the cycles of life. In dreams it can have a variety of other meanings, depending on the other elements: a full moon can be romantic if shared with a loved one, or it can act as a spotlight if you are trying to make a night-time escape. A new moon can symbolize depression, a crescent moon a smile. The moon is also most clearly seen at night, and its appearance in dreams may suggest secrecy, dark deeds, hidden things or the occult.

In your dream: Note the moon phase – is it crescent, full, waning, new? The moon often represents the three main stages of life – youth, adulthood and old age: how does this apply to you?

The moon has been seen as male in some eras, fickle, given to judging by appearances and inconstant, and in dreams may symbolize someone you should not trust.

Eclipse

An eclipse, a total solar eclipse in particular, can be an alarming experience: the sky darkens, the temperature drops, the birds stop singing and an eerie silence falls.

In your dream: Are you being 'eclipsed' in your waking life? Is someone deliberately trying to downplay your skills and ideas in order to advance their own?

Meteor

Meteors occupy two niches in the public consciousness – the beauty of a meteor shower and the fear of a devastating meteor impact.

In your dream: If you dreamed of a meteor shower this may symbolize both excitement for something rare and unusual, and flashes of inspiration that can lead to the successful completion of projects at work or home. If it was a meteor impact perhaps you fear something vast and completely out of your control to deal with, perhaps death, or the destruction of your personal world.

Comet

Although comets aren't particularly rare, it's not often that one approaches earth closely enough to provide a good display. Comets were originally perceived as foretelling, if not causing, disasters: these days we're more likely to spend hours outside enjoying the spectacle.

In your dream: A comet may indicate a revelation or insight that comes from an unexpected source. Alternatively it may symbolize a person of great enthusiasm or brilliance who comes into your life for a short while, brightening everything, then leaves again. Have you experienced a sudden revelation or exciting change in your waking life?

Planets

If the planets were those in our solar system, your subconscious may be linking them to their astrological meanings, especially if you are interested in the subject. They may indicate an area of your life that needs attention, or perhaps a person who embodies that planet's qualities.

Mercury – communication and travel
Venus – love and desire, relationships
Mars – anger, confrontation, war
Jupiter – work, learning, legal matters
Saturn – obstacles and difficulties, old age
Uranus – new experiences, new discoveries
Neptune – hidden things, secrets, psychological matters
Pluto – wealth of all kinds

In your dream: Were you living on or visiting an alien planet? In this case the dream is more likely to symbolize your own feelings of alienation – or alternatively a desire to be different, an eagerness to explore beyond your own boundaries, or a hankering for escape from a mundane waking life.

Stars

Stars generally symbolize a hope, wish or ambition.

In your dream: Are you 'reaching for the stars' in your waking life? Do you know someone who is 'a star', perhaps because of their strength or resilience? If you dream of a particular star, what does that mean to you? Is someone close to you your 'pole star', for example, around whom your life revolves? Sirius, the Dog Star, is one of the brightest in the sky – does it represent someone to you?

A happy dream of boarding a space vessel for an interplanetary journey combines excitement, a little fear and the joy of expanding your horizons. Alternatively, if you're forced onto the craft unwillingly, do you fear change, dread leaving behind the familiar, feel that control of your life has been taken from you?

(See also Spaceraft, page 202; Aliens, page 377)

Constellations

Early humans fancied they saw patterns in the sky, and peopled the heavens with their deities and heroes. We still know most of the constellations by their old names and shapes, and most people will be able to recognize at least a couple of star groups – Orion the Hunter or the Southern Cross, for example.

The changing positions of constellations have been used for millennia as guides for sailors, hunters and trackers.

In your dream: What constellations did you see – the traditional star groups, or did your mind create new ones? Were you imposing your hopes and dreams onto the stars in your sky, and if so, what images or stories did you create? Can you use them in your waking life?

Galaxies

Few people have any true concept of the remoteness and sizes of other galaxies, so for most they represent immeasurable distance, the fascination of the alien, and, influenced by films or photographs, great beauty.

In your dream: A dream of galaxies indicates a wish to explore far beyond the limits of human boundaries, whether physically or imaginatively. They symbolize optimism, expansion, adventure and the future – an open, positive and responsive mindset. Are you currently experiencing change in your waking life? Is it exciting? Do you feel hopeful?

Nebulae

Nebulae are clouds of gas and matter in space, some of them extremely beautiful. Most can't be seen with the naked eye, so our images of nebulae rely on pictures taken by astronomers. The significance of a nebula in a dream depends very much on its shape and colour.

In your dream: Did the nebula clearly resemble familiar objects – flowers, birds or insects – or was it more abstract? These shapes suggest that something hazy or not fully understood is blocking your path to the future.
(See also Colours, pages 255–259)

WEATHER

Sunshine

Bright sunny days make the world seem a brighter, happier place, and tend to have a cheering and heartening effect on everyone. The most usual meaning of sunshine in a dream is simply that – the dreamer's life is sunny and settled at the moment, free of any major problems.

In your dream: Did you feel unhappy despite the sunny weather? This can indicate a struggle to maintain a cheerful façade in the face of personal problems – laughing on the outside but crying inside. Did the dream present you with any ideas as to how to improve the situation?

Seeing the sun through clouds may indicate your subconscious awareness that although life may seem a little less than perfect at the moment, things will get better.

Rainbow

The rainbow has traditionally been seen as a bridge between heaven and earth, either a literal bridge (as in Bifrost, the mythical rainbow bridge connecting Midgard, the realm of man, with Asgard, the realm of the gods in Norse mythology) or as a symbolic bridge – as in God's promise to Noah.

In your dream: Is there a major issue you are focusing on in your waking life? Other images in your dream may indicate the issue to which the rainbow's relates and, in dreams, as in life, the rainbow is a symbol of hope – even if that hope is an impossible one, as in finding the pot of gold at the end of the rainbow!

(See also Bridge, page 323)

Rain

Rain comes in many guises, from the gentle spring shower to monsoon. It's an essential part of nature, bringing much needed water to growing plants. Rain can also 'clear the air', leaving everything clean and fresh in its wake. Its meaning in dreams is affected by whether you were protected or sheltered from the rain or not.

In your dream: Was it drizzle or a short shower? Are you finding little things – or other people – irritating at the moment? Perhaps simply confiding in a friend – a moaning session over a coffee or drink, for example – would be enough to release the stress!

If the rain was steady: are you 'under the weather' at the moment? Unhappy due to the breakdown of a relationship? Feeling unwell? Is there anything you can do to change the situation or is it simply a matter of time?

Hail

Hail is frozen rain. Add a cold and uncomfortable emotional environment to the meaning for rain, above.

In your dream: Was the hail simply inconvenient or a real impediment? Is someone you dislike 'hailing' you, asking you to do something unwelcome?

Thunder

There's a thunder god in most ancient religions – unsurprisingly, as hearing the sky growl is enough to startle even so-called sophisticated modern humans! By association, thunder has come to symbolize anger, specifically the anger of someone in authority.

In your waking life: Are you having problems with someone you see as your superior, whether at work or in other areas of your life? Have you made someone angry? Is it a passing storm or would it be in your best interests to try to resolve the issues before the situation worsens?

Storm, hurricane, typhoon

Being caught in a howling storm usually indicates you feel completely at the mercy of the elements, unable to exert any control over your waking life, especially in personal relationships.

In your waking life: Are you caught up in a stormy, passionate affair, or facing the prospect of such a relationship being ended by the other person? Whatever the reason, the feelings of helplessness created by such a dream, especially if it's recurrent, can easily carry over into your waking life, and it would be sensible to examine the source to see if there's any way to escape.

Lightning

While startling, lightning also illuminates – only for a fraction of a second, but enough to impress the surroundings on our memory. Symbolically, it forms a brilliant 'bridge' between heaven and earth, the realm of the mind and the imagination and the realm of the physical senses.

In your dream: What does the lightning reveal: dangers around you, or the way forwards? Is it a 'flash of inspiration' and, if so, how can you use it to best advantage?

Fog

Fog obscures. In dreams, it usually indicates that you are unable to discern the situation clearly, whether it's a relationship, a work project or someone's motives. Your subconscious may be warning you to proceed with extreme caution to prevent catastrophe.

In your waking life: Is there someone or something of which you need to be particularly wary?

Wind

From a light breeze to a strong wind, moving air lifts dust and blows away the cobwebs.

In your dream: Unaccompanied by any other strong weather image, wind may suggest you do something to lift yourself out of a rut, try something new and challenging. Do you currently feel in a rut or in need of change?

Snow

Snow softens edges, hides irregularities. It's very pretty, but can be deadly. Snow will have a different significance depending on your location. In areas where it rarely snows, dreaming of either enjoying the novelty or being caught in a blizzard will be more noteworthy than if you regularly live with snowy conditions for part of the year.

In your dream: Were you walking through deep snow? This suggests that you be wary of unseen obstacles and pitfalls. Sitting inside in the warm watching snow fall suggests contentment. Dreaming of struggling through a blizzard is similar to struggling through a storm [see page 44] with the added danger of sub-zero emotional temperature, a sense of isolation and abandonment, and complete lack of any friendly assistance.

EXTREMES

Flood

Floods are potentially life-threatening. The water symbolism may reflect a profound level of emotional turmoil.

In your waking life: Are you being swept away or drowned, or in danger of losing everything you possess, because of a dangerously intense relationship? Consider if it's really worth it.
(See also Water, page 63 and watery symbols such as River and Sea earlier in this chapter)

Drought

Droughts signify the loss of all that is essential for life and growth. The absence of water can symbolize lack of emotion, a barrenness in your life.

In your waking life: Do you feel completely drained, without emotion at all, due to personal crisis or in the aftermath of an affair? Or is that the best way to deal with everything that's happening in your waking life? It can be a perilous strategy, and emotional recovery can take a long time.

Sandstorm

Being literally 'sand-blasted' is a very painful experience – although it can expose the fresh and new below the surface.

In your waking life: Have you been or are you likely to be the subject of a 'tongue-lashing' by another person? Was it delivered out of the blue and/or by a friend?

Tornado

Tornadoes form swiftly, wreak enormous damage and harm, and usually dissipate as suddenly as they started.

In your waking life: Is your subconscious warning you of the probable disastrous outcome of a proposed source of action – or brief affair?

TREES

Apple tree

A powerful image, the apple tree has been seen as 'the tree of the knowledge of good and evil' planted in the Garden of Eden. Apples and apple trees symbolize common sense and an instinctive awareness of your physical body, its health and weaknesses. A healthy, fruitful tree suggests good health or the road to it.

In your dream: Was the tree solitary or growing in an orchard? The former may suggest you see yourself as a loner and take responsibility for your own health, while the latter indicates a more gregarious nature that prefers the support of others in health-related matters.

Were you picking apples from the tree? Did you pick an apple yourself or did someone pick it for you, and if so, who? Is your subconscious suggesting you are being tempted to do something against your better judgement – or simply that you wish to share your knowledge with another?

(See also Apple, page 263)

Holly

The glossy leaves and bright red berries of holly have brightened the winter season since time immemorial. It's a cheerful, cheering symbol, symbolizing protection and the lifting of spirits in times of darkness.

In your dream: Is there a trying issue in your waking life you hope will be resolved soon? Your subconscious may be telling you not to despair, you can cope, and matters will improve. Alternatively, if you celebrate the winter solstice in some way – Christmas, Yule, Hanukah – and it's drawing close, you could just be reminding yourself to start preparing!

Oak

Emblematic of strength and endurance in several cultures, the oak is also a symbol of England and the English. Its appearance may indicate the country itself, especially if it's by itself.

In your dream: Are you under or touching the tree? This may suggest either that you need a 'heart of oak' in order to deal with your current situation, or that you feel sheltered and protected from harm.

Dreaming of acorns indicates that it's time to put your plans into action – plant the seeds so great things may grow from them.

Fir

Fir trees, with their sturdy, upreaching conical shape and dense foliage, are familiar to most of us as Yule or Christmas trees. They represent the power to resist change, to endure through the bad times.

In your dream: Was the tree decorated? If so, are you looking forward to a forthcoming event, or are you anxious and unprepared? Did it make you feel nostalgic? If so, is your mind nudging you to think about past times or people with whom you have lost touch? An undecorated tree in a household or Yuletide setting may suggest you feel you have nothing to celebrate.

Pine

Pine trees, while used as Yule trees, are also well known for their fresh scent and strongly disinfectant essential oil. The beautiful pale wood is used for a huge number of purposes in construction and furniture making. The sculptural shape of some varieties can be of relevance in a dream.

In your dream: Was it a solitary Scots pine, strong and silent – representing someone you know? A Western white pine, tall and narrow like a ladder to the sky, suggesting your wish to climb higher in life? Or a bristlecone pine, possibly the longest-lived of all trees, a survivor in the face of overwhelming odds?

Eucalyptus

Native to Australia, the eucalyptus is known throughout the world for its oil, which is a powerful disinfectant and extremely useful in alleviating respiratory problems of all kinds. Many florists use it in arrangements since it has beautiful silvery bluish leaves, striking and unusual to anyone only used to green foliage. Unless you have visited or live in Australia – or have the tree planted in your garden – dreaming of a eucalyptus suggests that something may be out of place in your life.

In your waking life: Do you feel comfortable where you are? Do you have 'room to breathe'? Would you feel happier somewhere else – even a different country? Or do you simply yearn for something to make your life more interesting?

Japanese maple

A graceful tree, with leaves in a fabulous range of colours, this maple symbolizes the sophistication of Japan and is more robust than it appears. In dreams, the maple may symbolize the country itself, especially if it's in the form of a bonsai, or indicate a tranquil frame of mind, particularly if it's beside water.

In your dream: If you're unable to reach the tree, or if it's in a sickly state, your subconscious may be suggesting that you are yearning for beauty and serenity in your life.
(See also Countries and Continents, pages 32–35)

Canadian maple

The maple tree is so much a part of Canada's heart that a maple leaf appears on the national flag. This elegant tree is at its most beautiful in autumn, when the colours of the leaves fill the land with blazing colour. Dreaming of autumn maples suggests a deep inner desire for more colour in your life, both physically and metaphorically.

In your waking life: Do you feel dull and colourless, or that you are leading a dull life? Consider how you can brighten up, taking your inspiration from nature.

Palm

Unless you live where palm trees grow, palms of all kinds usually suggest the romance of idyllic desert islands, hot lazy days on the beach or swimming in warm, clear tropical waters. Dreaming of palms usually indicates a desire for just such a release, a return to a simpler, more relaxed life far from the complications of modern life.

However, **storm-tossed palms** are associated with feelings of fear or loss, indicating that you may fear being 'deserted', abandoned or 'cast adrift'.

In your waking life: Are you in a failing relationship? Are there problems at work – perhaps changes being made to the workforce and you fear being left behind? Is it time for you to take a break?

Baobab

The baobab is native to Africa and looks as though it's been planted upside down: the branches are bare for three quarters of each year and look like a root system. The tree is extremely tenacious, can live to an immense age and reach a massive size. Known as the 'tree of life', every part of the tree is useful, from the vitamin C-rich fruit to the water stored in its trunk to its fire-resistant bark.

In your dream: If you have seen a baobab in waking life, its appearance in a dream most likely urges you to consider something important or striking that happened at that time. If you have only seen pictures of the tree, its surreal form may be prompting you to literally turn things upside down, look at your life and any attendant problems from a completely new perspective!

Willow

The willow is a graceful tree, at its best near water: it has an artistic, somewhat melancholic reputation, especially the weeping willow. Depending on your emotions, its appearance in dreams may suggest either pining after a loved one, an inner need to satisfy a frustrated artistic urge or a desire to take a break from the demands of daily life.

In your dream: Were you trapped in a willow's branches? This may indicate you feel someone – a friend or family member – is taking advantage of you, pretending to be helpless or dependent in order to avoid taking responsibility.

Redwood

The American sequoia is an ancient species. It's a giant, a skyscraper among trees.

In your dream: If you have seen redwoods in your waking life, remember the circumstances. Were they happy? Are the dream redwoods a symbol of a great holiday, or did their majesty perhaps speak to something within you? How might that apply to your current situation?

If you've never seen one, to dream of redwoods, especially if you are feeling afraid or threatened in the dream, suggests that you feel overwhelmed by things outside your control. Conversely, if you feel safe, you probably feel protected by your environment and the people who matter to you.
(See also American Continent, page 33; Emotions, pages 130–134)

Yew

Yews grow very slowly, and can live to an immense age – several thousand years if left undisturbed. The tree has been associated with immortality for millennia, although its presence in many graveyards has also led to it being linked with death – the leaves and seeds are toxic to humans and some animals.

In your dream: Was the setting dark and gloomy? The presence of yews may suggest morbid fears. If such dreams recur frequently for no obvious reason, your subconscious might be warning you of some underlying problem: it might be wise to see a doctor or counsellor.

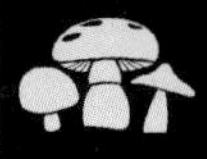

PLANTS

Violet

Violets are charming flowers with an old-fashioned reputation. Are you a 'shrinking violet', shy and unsure of yourself, unwilling to draw attention to yourself?

In your dream: What happened to the flower? If it was trampled underfoot, it's a clear warning to take positive action if you don't wish to have the same happen to you.

Rose

Roses, especially red roses, with their velvety petals, rich colours and delicious scent, are often given as an expression of love. In dreams, they can signify love, but they can also suggest hidden threats: rose thorns can be vicious things, and dreaming of being pricked can indicate that while everything may seem 'rosy' on the surface, underneath there may be niggling problems.

In your dream: Who gave you the roses, or did you present them to someone else? If the latter, was it someone unexpected or a stranger? This may indicate that you are dissatisfied with your current emotional attachments and tempted to try something new.

Orchid

Orchids are beautiful, exotic and difficult to grow without the correct conditions.

In your dream: Was the orchid presented as gift? This indicates that the giver views the receiver as something rare and precious, to be treasured and cared for with respect.

Lily

Lilies are often used in churches and funeral decorations, and have a sombre reputation.

In your waking life: Is something serious happening in your life, events that may have unpleasant consequences?

Mistletoe

The plant is a parasite, often growing on apple trees, and an ancient fertility symbol: kissing under the mistletoe – the well-established Yuletide tradition – is a talismanic wish for a successful sex-life and healthy children!

In your dream: Who did you dream of kissing? If it wasn't your partner, it may be someone to whom you feel strongly attracted, even if you're unwilling to act on the desire.

Ivy

Ivy is renowned for its climbing and clinging qualities. A dream featuring ivy prominently indicates that someone is being clingy.

In your dream: Who does the ivy represent? In your waking life are you being too dependent on someone else, or are they relying too heavily on you? A dream of ivy being cut or torn down should be taken as a warning to the clinger to amend their behaviour before someone else takes away their emotional or financial support.

Daisy

Often called the 'children's flower', daisies are childhood favourites for many, the petals plucked to the chant of 'he loves me, he loves me not', the flowers themselves made into daisy chains.

In your waking life: Are you feeling 'fresh as a daisy' at the moment? A dream prominently featuring daisies suggests that your life is progressing smoothly and happily. Giving daisies to someone indicates innocent, playful affection rather than physical love or lust.

Thistle

The thistle is the national emblem of Scotland, and is a tough, hardy plant able to grow almost anywhere.

In your waking life: Are you dealing with a 'prickly personality'? Alternatively, thistles may represent problems, minor but aggravating and difficult to solve.

Thorns

Thorns in a dream symbolize difficulties to be overcome: how best to deal with them may be illustrated by the action you took.

In your dream: Did you cut them down? Direct action at the source may be the answer. If you forced your way through them, perhaps simply gritting your teeth and putting up with the problem is the best course. Avoiding them completely might work in the short term, but many thorns spread by underground suckers, only to resurface elsewhere: dealing with the problem now will save it re-emerging in the future. (See also Rose, page 57)

Fern

Ferns are very ancient, and grow best in shady places.

In your waking life: Are you involved in 'shady dealing' at the moment? Fern 'seed' had a reputation for making things invisible – do you wish you could disappear to avoid an awkward situation? Or do you prefer to remain in the background, out of the limelight?

Moss

'A rolling stone gathers no moss'.

In your waking life: Are you forever on the move, dashing about, running yourself into the ground and never taking a much-needed rest?

Toadstool, mushroom

Toadstools are poisonous, though many are pretty, and mushrooms flourish in the dark; some grow in manure. Dreaming of the former may be a warning to be wary of interesting but unfamiliar objects, while the latter are nutritious, but grow best undisturbed.

In your waking life: Are you involved with something that would progress best if left to develop by itself? Do you need to face up to the unpleasant realities of a situation in order to appreciate its outcome?

Nettle

The fine hairs on the nettle's leaves and stem are the source of its stinging abilities.

In your waking life: Are there problems to be battled? These difficulties will leave a sting behind and have repercussions that may last for a while.

THE ELEMENTS

Fire

Fire is both welcoming and dangerous. Its meaning in a dream depends entirely on the context.

In your dream: A cosy fire in a hearth on a cold day is comforting and suggests you are happy with the way your life is progressing. Camp-fires represent a way to cook and keep warm while in the open, and may have the additional aspect of holiday excitement. A candle symbolizes light in the darkness and enlightenment. A raging forest fire can indicate that in waking life you're surrounded by inflamed passions – lust or anger – which could prove very dangerous for your emotional or physical health. It can also be a symbol of your willpower, especially if you're controlling the fire in some way.

Water

Water generally represents the spirit, and more particularly emotion: both can quench thirst, cleanse and refresh, and drench or drown you, depending on context.

In your dream: What form did the water take? Were you engulfed by it, enjoying it or using it in a practical way? Was it life-restoring or life-threatening?
(See also Sea, page 29; Lake, page 27 and other watery places earlier in this chapter; Plumber, page 171; Swimming, page 213; Weather, pages 42–46)

Earth

Earth – soil – represents rootedness, groundedness, in dreams. It symbolizes physical objects and concerns, physical growth and wealth of experience as well as the potential for financial wealth.

In your dream: Were you digging? This usually indicates searching for something buried, often within yourself.
(See also Gardener, page 174; Farmer, page 173)

Air

Air symbolizes the imagination, aspiration, hopes and ambitions. Any dream which features air prominently will involve these aspects of your life.

In your dream: Was the air your element – were you flying? Or were you battling against suffocation? A lack of air may equate to a lack of imagination or ambition in your waking life, which can result in the stagnation of development.
(See also Pilot, page 200; Flying, page 143)

GEMS AND METALS

If the jewel or metal is in the form of jewellery in the dream, see also Jewellery, page 292.

Diamond

As well as being the most expensive gemstone on the planet, diamond is also the hardest. As such it has become a symbol of endurance, strength and eternity. In a ring – engagement or eternity ring, for example – it symbolizes everlasting love and devotion. A 'rough diamond', unpolished or still embedded in rock, probably represents someone you know and feel attracted to, despite or because of their unrefined nature. To have unset diamonds in your hands represents physical wealth, and is probably a wish-fulfilment dream.

In your dream: What form did the gem take? Was something in the dream made of diamond? If so, refer to the subject entry in the appropriate part of the book, then consider why you perceived it being made of diamonds. Is it something very precious to you? Something or someone hard, cold and impenetrable? If it was a tool, do you need it to open, build or break something so heavily locked and guarded that nothing short of the hardest mineral on earth will suffice?

Ruby

The rich redness of rubies often represent blood, or the emotions of the heart – love, lust and passion.

In your dream: Worn as jewellery, rubies symbolize banked passion. Giving or receiving a ruby often indicates hidden lust directed towards the recipient, and can indicate that the giver is willing to fight to gain the other's love.

Sapphire

Beautiful, sky-blue sapphire was traditionally believed to quench the fires of passion, and represents tranquillity, open-mindedness, the search for knowledge.

In your dream: Sapphires can symbolize platonic love and like-minded friendship.

Emerald

Rich green emerald is reputed to calm the mind and nerves, and promote truth. Emeralds can also symbolize the richness of the earth and its natural treasures.

In your dream: Receiving an emerald suggests that the provider would like to 'give you the earth' as a gift.

Tiger's eye

This golden semi-precious gem is described as chatoyant – having a changing , undulating lustre like a cat's eye. Often used for men's signet rings, it was once worn by ancient Roman soldiers for protection in battle – the beautiful play of light was reputed to deceive the eye, making the warrior more difficult to hit.

In your dream: Tiger's eye symbolizes royalty, the sun and the qualities of the tiger.
(See also Tiger, page 80)

Jade

Jade is mainly known as an oriental stone, but it was also used by the Aztec and Incan peoples. It's been considered valuable for thousands of years (its Chinese name mean 'precious'). The best known and most desirable jade is a beautiful soft green colour.

In your dream: Jade may suggest precious things, nostalgia, gentleness and taking pleasure in nature's treasures.

Pearl

Pearls have been worn as jewellery for at least five millennia, and were originally worn as symbols of wealth, authority and good fortune. They are also symbolic of feminine beauty and purity – although they do have a reputation for being unlucky for brides, perhaps because they are created with pain and their removal from the shell causes the oyster's death. Other traditions accord them the ability to give the wearer long life. There's a legend that Cleopatra dissolved pearls in a cup of wine in order to seduce Mark Antony, something of an expensive aphrodisiac. (Pearls don't dissolve in wine, but they will in vinegar, though that's nothing like as romantic!)

In your dream: Pearls can symbolize tears or regrets, especially if worn or given by someone now dead. Alternatively, pearls given by a lover symbolize respectful love.

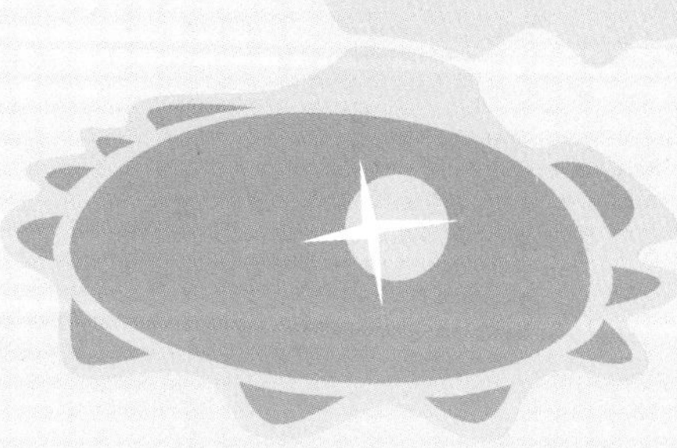

Opal

Opals are fragile, and their beautiful play of delicate colours can become dulled if they come into contact with grease, which has led to their reputation of being unlucky.

In your dream: Opals can indicate unsolved mysteries in your life, flashes of insight and changes of fortune.

Amber

The solidified resin from prehistoric pines often has seeds or occasionally small insects embedded in it. It's been described as solid sunlight for its golden colour, and is warm to the touch.

In your dream: Amber usually symbolizes the past as seen through a nostalgic haze: home, the security of a happy childhood and the warmth of summer.

Turquoise

Turquoise has an association with Amerindian culture, and may represent a link to the spiritual qualities of unity with nature. Its lovely colour has been likened to holding a piece of the sky in your hands.

In your dream: Turquoise may indicate calmness and serenity, a happy and relaxed outlook on life.

Moonstone

So-called because of its beautiful shimmering translucent whiteness, moonstone is considered a magical stone, and is used to promote sweet and beneficial dreams in some cultures, intuition and tenderness in others.

In your dream: A moonstone generally indicates fluidity, change, versatility – its appearance may herald a journey, or the arrival of a lover.

Gold

There's an almost magical quality to gold: it's known as the purest of metals, incorruptible and highly valuable. In dreams it indicates wealth, nobility, generosity and expansiveness. It can also represent greed and miserliness if it's being hoarded. Gold traditionally also represents the sun, and thus warmth and growth.

In your dream: Have you been 'as good as gold'? Do you have a 'golden touch', somehow bringing to successful fruition everything you do? Or is the dream warning you that 'all that glisters is not gold', to be careful not to be too trusting or too gullible, or take things at face value?

Silver

Whereas gold represents the sun, silver represents the moon. It's a malleable metal, easily worked into a multitude of shapes, and in dreams may suggest flexibility. It's also a protective talisman, particularly against supernatural creatures and hostile influences.

In your dream: Were you wearing silver jewellery in the shape of a religious symbol? This suggests you feel the need to protect yourself from someone or something subtly threatening you in waking life. Are you being subjected to emotional blackmail at home or at work?
(See also Moon, page 37; religious symbols in Ritual, Ceremony and Celebration, page 352–367)

Platinum

This precious metal is much rarer than gold, It's silver-coloured but brighter than silver and doesn't tarnish. It has been known for millennia, but only appeared in the public consciousness in the 18th century when if began to be used in jewellery. Platinum symbolizes purity and uniqueness and is not a common image in dreams.

In your dream: To be given platinum indicates that the giver considers you 'one of a kind' and worth the kind of love that expresses itself in subtle, refined wealth.

Steel

Steel is used everywhere, in construction, in manufacturing, in daily life, even in jewellery.

In your dream: Steel's cool, sleek beauty may suggest that you need to be as 'strong as steel' without losing control of your emotional balance – or your temper.

Copper

Copper's beautiful colour and ability to conduct electricity efficiently make it an interesting image in dreams.

In your dream: What form did the copper take? A lightning conductor may associate it with the need to deflect someone's anger, especially if the metal was worn as jewellery in the dream. Its rich colour may symbolize autumn, or the hair of a hot-tempered individual, or a somewhat ferocious, bruising passion.

Lead

Lead is toxic, but it's also incredibly dense, used to protect the frail human body from the radiation that would destroy it from the inside out. In dreams it indicates the need to shield yourself from the 'fall-out' of extreme unpleasantness in your waking life.

In your waking life: Do you have 'lead in your boots', finding it difficult to get yourself moving? Or do you have a 'lead-lined stomach', able to digest food that would give others unpleasant digestive complaints?

Iron

Iron was one of the earliest metals to be worked, taking over from the softer bronze (an alloy of copper and tin). Its strength and rigidity made it ideal for tools and weapons such as knives and axes.

In your dream: Is your subconscious warning you about people trying to take advantage of you? Or are you finding it necessary to be 'hard as iron' in your waking life? Or do you need to be 'iron-fisted', make your voice heard even if you have to hammer the table to do it?
(See also Blacksmith, page 189)

2 CREATURES

Over time, many animals have acquired special significance and regularly appear in people's dreams. Sometimes their appearance is insignificant, but if a specific creature features prominently, it could be symbolic. Remember that real-life experience will influence meaning in a dream. If you seldom encounter a snake in your waking life, a dream appearance is likely to be symbolic, but if you keep snakes, a dream about the health of one may indicate something amiss that your subconscious has noticed. Fantasy and mythological creatures can be found in the Supernatural section, page 368.

DOMESTIC ANIMALS

Cat

Cats have always been viewed as magical, from the Egyptian worship of them through the fear of witches' familiars to the affectionate, soothing moggies of today. Their ability to extricate themselves from the most perilous conditions, which led to the 'nine lives' belief, their independence, grace, skill in hunting and occasional casual cruelty make them entirely different from every other animal we know.

If you like or own cats, a cat in a dream is going to indicate something favourable; if you dislike or are afraid of cats, the opposite will apply.

In your dream: What is the cat doing, what is its size and colour, where is it, and what is its attitude towards you? Is it an aspect of yourself or an outside force? A threat, or an opportunity? Consider cat myths and legends from your own nationality as well as what the cat means to you personally.

Dog

Dogs have enjoyed a special, if subservient, relationship with humans since they were first domesticated from wolves. They are pack animals, instinctively accepting their owner as the leader of the pack, and from sheepdog to show dog, sled-pulling husky to guide-dog, or just as the faithful, affectionate family pet, dogs are very useful creatures. It's no wonder they're called 'man's best friend'.

In your dream: Who does the dog represent? What was the animal doing – running away from you, fetching, guiding you through uncertain territory? Did you trust it, or were you afraid that it might turn and attack you like a '**mad dog**'?

Horse

Powerful, resolute, intelligent, throughout history the horse has been a close friend of humanity. All around the world, in myth as in life, the animal represents the act of travelling, of delivering goods or people from one place to another.

In your dream: Were you **riding** the horse? This symbolizes travelling towards your goal: if it's a smooth ride, all is going well; if not, you anticipate problems. Riding alone indicates you prefer to do things your own way, while in a group means working in a team is important to you. If the horse was running away from you, you feel that opportunities are racing away; running towards you and you see opportunities approaching, but you'll need to grab them and hold on tight. (See also Horseriding, page 216)

Donkey

The donkey has been used as a beast of burden for thousands of years. Hardy, tough and strong, it's notable for its ability to carry large, heavy loads and for its stubbornness, and symbolizes either or both of these qualities in dreams.

In your dream: Does the animal represent you or someone else? Are you carrying a heavy load, especially at work, or are you expecting others to do it for you? Alternatively, are you being 'mulish' about a particular matter, person or situation? Is someone else behaving in such a way towards you? Is this stubbornness an issue of pride, of refusing to compromise? What were the other circumstances in the dream? Or perhaps the dream was telling you to stop being 'an ass' about something?

Lamb

Lambs generally symbolize spring, the young and playfulness. In dreams they may express the laughter-loving side of your nature, the joy of new beginnings.

In your dream: The lamb may also represent Jesus in the aspect of the **sacrificial lamb**, whose blood is spilt on behalf of the 'flock' of believers. If this is the meaning in your dream, what emotion accompanied the image? Hope, relief, guilt, sadness, anger or gratitude? What does this reveal about your religious leanings?
(See also Shepherd, page 173)

Hare

Hares are much less common than rabbits, and have an association with the moon.

In your dream: Their appearance is often associated with the saying 'mad as a March hare' and may be either a warning about acting irresponsibly, or advising you to relax and play a little, depending on your feeling while dreaming.

Pig

Our language is rich in pig imagery: as greedy as a pig, pig-ignorant (although pigs are clever animals), a room as dirty as a pig-sty. But pigs can be happy – living 'high on the 'hog' or being 'pigs in clover'.

In your dream: Are you 'making a pig of yourself'? Is someone close to you behaving like a pig? Are you 'wallowing in the mud' – is it time to clean up the mess?

Rabbit

The rabbit's usually docile nature, softness and innocently cute appeal makes it a good pet for children; at the same time, it's a well-known symbol of fertility. Carrying a rabbit's foot is supposed to bring good luck.

In your dream: Was the rabbit a symbol from your childhood? Was it accompanied by a feeling of nostalgia, happiness or misery? It may represent a wish to return to an easier, more innocent time, especially if your waking life is fraught. Alternatively, if your early life was unhappy, the dream may suggest a need to sort out unresolved issues from your past.

If there were so many rabbits you felt overwhelmed, is your subconscious suggesting that you have too many ideas/projects on the go and may need to cut back a little? However, if you felt excited or happy, perhaps your mind is reassuring you that you can cope.

A dream of **dead** or dying rabbits suggests a fear of your projects failing. It might be wise to reappraise matters.

Cow

Cows symbolize the passive nurturing principle. They produce milk while alive, and meat and leather when dead, so almost every part of the animal is valuable.

In your dream: To see live cows indicates a measure of satisfaction with the way your life is going, confidence that you have everything you need to survive comfortably. **Dead cows** suggest an awareness that your lifestyle is under threat. **Bulls** may represent 'bullish', stubborn or threatening people in your waking life.

WILD ANIMALS

Lion

The lion can represent both a magnificent wild animal, the king of the beasts, and the tragedy of a caged animal in a zoo or circus.

In your dream: Did the lion represent an element of yourself – your powers of leadership, for example, or your compassion, your 'lion-heartedness'? Or was it someone else, someone you respect or see as an authority figure? What was the animal doing? Can you work out how this relates to what's happening in your life?

Tiger

Tigers are the biggest of the cats, solitary, powerful, beautiful, implacable, unpredictable and dangerous. They have resonance with the mysteries of India, and may indicate a profound personal inner strength.

In your dream: Was the tiger being hunted or in a cage? If so, the dream suggests that you may feel yourself under siege from jealous people around you.

Jaguar

The jaguar symbolizes concealed strength, patience, sleekness and agility.

In your waking life: Do you feel yourself lacking in these qualities? This may especially be the case if the cat was walking away from you, or appearing to lead you.

Cheetah

The cheetah represents the speed of the successful hunter, and is the fastest land animal on the planet.

In your waking life: Is your subconscious urging you to move faster, to escape, or chase down something – opportunities, a new relationship? Are you in control of the cheetah, or is it hunting you?

Wolf

Wolves have a somewhat ambivalent reputation. On the one hand they're seen as romantic creatures, on the other as predators. The meaning of the image in the dream will depend on your view of the animal, what it means to you. Do you see wolves as survivors, noble, faithful animals? Wise guides? Vicious killers? Co-operative pack animals?

In your dream: If you dreamt of a solitary wolf, do you feel yourself to be a 'lone wolf', elusive and self-reliant? Or are you afraid someone is trying to muscle in on something you perceive as yours – a lover, perhaps? If the dream involved a **pack of wolves**, were you running with them or being threatened by them? Consider what this means in relation to how you feel about the animal. Is there a part of yourself that strives for the perceived freedom and wildness of the wolf, or are you being chased by a pack of snapping, howling problems in your waking life?

Fox

The fox has a reputation for slyness and cleverness, whether for escaping from the hunter or stealing the chickens from the henhouse. It's an admirably adaptable animal, and attractive, with its bushy tail and bright eyes.

In your dream: What was the fox doing? Moving furtively, trying to hide, or walking with confidence? Was the fox an aspect of yourself, or is your subconscious warning you to be wary of someone who intends you harm – perhaps by spreading rumours or lies about you?

Hyena

Hyenas are scavengers, feeding on the kill of other animals.

In your dream: To dream of hyenas, especially if you've never seen them in your waking life, suggests that something has left you feeling helpless, surrounded by people who are more than willing to 'take a bite' out of you.

Monkey

Apes of all kinds can be seen as disturbingly close to human in shape and behaviour.

In your dream: What were they doing? Is your subconscious warning you not to 'monkey around', to behave with a little more decorum? Or do you feel that you're surrounded by chattering, imitative monkeys?

Deer

Swift, graceful, sure-footed and wary, deer represent an inner self that yearns for freedom and is uneasy with the modern world.

In your dream: If the deer is being hunted, you may feel under threat, if you are hunting it yourself, the dream indicates either the desire to suppress your inner self in order to blend in with society, or the fear that society is forcing you to stifle your real self. Dreaming of a proud **stag** suggests a secret desire for a more primitive, earthy kind of sexual intimacy.

Camel

Sometimes known as 'the ship of the desert', the camel is an odd-looking but extremely useful animal. Its reputation as bad-tempered and difficult to handle is outweighed by its strength, stamina and ability to go for long spells without a drink, using the water stored in its humps.

In your dream: A camel in a dream may suggest you'll find help in dealing with problems from a most unlikely – and possibly disliked – source.

Bear

Symbolizing gentle strength and sagacity, bears have been revered since prehistoric times.

In your dream: A bear **defending** you indicates that you feel yourself safe and protected from the worries of the world. However, if the bear is attacking you or yours, you feel, possibly subconsciously, that you're under threat from someone overpowering and relentless. Running from a bear suggests that you fear authority figures. Dreaming of a **hibernating bear** indicates a need to retire from the world to recharge your batteries!

Elephant

Currently the largest land animal in existence, elephants can represent a variety of difference things: devotion, wisdom, hard work, an excellent memory – 'an elephant never forgets' – or a ruinously useless possession, the 'white elephant' that you can't get rid of because you don't want to offend the person who gave it to you, but which costs an enormous amount to care for.

In your dream: Whatever the elephant represents to you, one aspect remains obvious: it's too big a creature to ignore easily, and whatever it symbolizes in your dream will be something equally large and important to you.

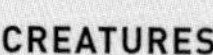

Giraffe

The tallest living land creature, giraffes feed on leaves from the upper branches of trees.

In your dream: If giraffes are the focus of the dream and you aren't familiar with them in waking life, it suggests a need to be free of the clutter on the ground in order to be able to see into the distance, most likely the future.

Rhinoceros

This solitary, thick-skinned, short-sighted and short-tempered herbivore has become something of a metaphor for quick-tempered, dim-witted belligerence.

In your dream: Dreaming of one, especially if it's **charging** towards you, may suggest you see someone in your life acting this way. Are they directly affecting you, your work or your self-confidence? What do you do to the rhino in the dream – **sidestep, run** or drive away, or **shoot** it? What does this tell you about how to improve matters?

Bat

For all their small size and general harmlessness to humans, bats are still viewed with fear and dislike. Yet they're fascinating creatures, the only mammal that can truly fly, and they use sonar to gauge distance and find their prey. They are considered lucky in China, and symbolize long life in other cultures. They appear at dusk, and tend to live in colonies in caves or other dark places, safely tucked away from the sunlight.

In your dream: Did the bat (or bats) scare you, swoop over and around you? If so it may represent a particular personal fear. Did it symbolize blindness, or a fear of the dark (or rather, the things that can sneak up on you in the dark), or possibly a fear of losing your way – something that rarely happens to bats?

What sort of bat did you see? The little countryside bat of temperate zones, the vampire bat of South America, or the fox-headed fruit-eating bat of the tropics? How did they make you feel? Do you associate bats with witches or evil? What were the other elements of the dream?

Rat

Rats have a reputation for being dirty, disease-carrying creatures, and it's true that most rats live in filthy surroundings where it's easy to pick up ailments that are life-threatening to humans. However, they're also fairly intelligent, adaptable, and can make good pets. The significance of rats in dreams depends on your view of them.

In your dream: Were you dreaming of 'a rat', a lover who betrayed you? Was it a horde of rats moving together, 'rats leaving a sinking ship', perhaps? The latter may suggest a subconscious awareness of problems with a relationship or work. Rats in your home suggests you may be feeling guilty about your standards of cleanliness: a rat at work, that you 'smell a rat' and someone may be trying to undermine you.

Squirrel

The squirrel usually symbolizes thrift and the wisdom of saving, both money and resources, for hard times to come.

In your dream: Dreaming of squirrels suggest an unconscious awareness that you may not be as prepared for the future as you thought, and warns you to reappraise your finances.

Mouse

Mice are seen as both industrious workers and pests. They're cautious and opportunistic, fast-moving yet inconspicuous creatures.

In your dream: Mice may indicate those who work behind the scenes, either to make everything run smoothly, or to destroy it. Are you being 'as quiet as a mouse'?

Ferret

Ferrets, and other muscovids such as weasels and stoats, are very unfairly associated with sneakiness, deceitfulness and underhanded activities.

In your dream: These animals usually suggest a subconscious warning that someone near you is untrustworthy and possibly trying to replace you.

Mole

Highly destructive little animals that live and hunt underground. In dreams, they symbolize forces at work 'underground' or in secret. It's no surprise that the term is used to refer to a spy working in one organization but passing confidential information to another organization.

In your dream: Perhaps in your waking life you feel someone is working against you, secretly and behind the scenes. But if you were a mole yourself in the dream, are you doing something unethical against someone else, without their knowledge?

Dreaming of **molehills** may signify nothing more than an unknown irritant in your life – someone playing 'pranks' that you find annoying.

BIRDS

Magpie

Magpies have a reputation for liking shiny things, which has led to them being seen as thieves. A single magpie is considered to be unlucky, mainly because magpies mate for life, so seeing one alone normally means its mate is dead. Two together, however, can indicate a happy, permanent relationship.

In your dream: Has someone been stealing from you? Or have you been helping yourself to others' property? How many magpies there were may also be significant ('One for sorrow, two for joy...').

Crow

Crows traditionally symbolize death, and are an unhappy image in a dream.

In your dream: Has someone or something – a relationship or job, perhaps – recently shown signs of ending? Or are you worried that it might do so, but are refusing to accept the possibility?

Dove

Doves are intimately associated with Aphrodite, the Greek goddess of love, and by extension represent love itself. A white dove is also a sign of peace and hope.

In your dream: Doves are a common image in your dreams if you are in love. The dove may also represent the Holy Spirit in the Christian faith, especially if you are a believer.

Cuckoo

The cuckoo's distinctive cry is a welcome harbinger of spring, but they will lay their eggs in other birds' nests at the expense of the original eggs. Having a cuckoo in the nest means supporting a demanding outsider encroaching on your home, and 'cuckoo' also relates to cuckold.

In your dream: Are you 'two-timing' your lover or are they doing the same to you?

Robin

The 'gardener's friend', this small, inquisitive, friendly bird has become a symbol of Yuletide, and is much loved.

In your dream: In a dream, the bird may be trying to show or tell you something to your benefit.

Eagle

Eagles symbolize freedom, far-sightedness and majesty. They are frequently found on military regalia, battle flags and as national symbols.

In your dream: Dreaming of an eagle flying high indicates self-confidence and strong motivation. A caged and miserable eagle, however, symbolizes powerful forces holding you back from achieving your dreams.

Owl

These birds traditionally represent wisdom – Athene, the Greek goddess of wisdom, often took the form of an owl.

In your dream: Does the bird symbolize someone you respect, whose advice you follow? Or are you considered an authority, looked up to by those around you?

Gull

Noisy, quarrelsome gulls often represent either the family or the workplace.

In your dream: An appearance in your dream may suggest that you need to escape for a while, for some peace and quiet!

Hawk, falcon

These are small, fast hunters.

In your dream: Birds of prey can indicate the need for stealth and bursts of energy to achieve your goals.

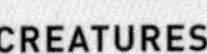

Pelican

With their large pouch under their bills, pelicans were traditionally considered to represent motherhood.

In your dream: If you associate pelicans with motherhood in your waking life, they may do the same in a dream, but they're more likely to indicate you've bitten off more than you can chew!

Penguin

Penguins tend to be comic figures, but are also famed for their ability to live and breed successfully in some of the most inhospitable places on earth.

In your dream: Dreaming of penguins suggests you feel that you're 'under siege', emotionally or mentally, but managing to cope. Does the dream indicate any way to alleviate the situation, make life more comfortable for yourself?

Swan

Swans epitomize elegance, yet their snow-white calmness is supported by energetic paddling beneath the water. They are also renowned for mating for life.

In your dream: Are you practising 'swan management', seemingly gliding serenely through life, while underneath you're working frantically to keep up? Or are you preparing your 'swansong', one last show of brilliance before you exit your current job, home or relationship? A pair of swans 'dancing' on the water may indicate a loving, long-term relationship.

Duck

Ducks traditionally symbolize fidelity and family life.

In your dream: Dreams of feeding them indicate your awareness that anything of worth needs nurturing – in body and mind – to keep it healthy.

Peacock

The peacock is probably the showiest bird on the planet, its name a byword for vanity and noisy self-aggrandisement.

In your dream: Who does the bird represent in the dream? Yourself or someone else? Is it a warning that behaving like a peacock will lead to someone's downfall?

Ostrich

These enormous, powerful birds have the odd reputation of burying their heads in the sand when danger threatens.

In your dream: Dreaming of an ostrich may suggest that you, or someone close to you, is doing the same, ignoring or denying approaching hazards. It would be sensible to 'take your head out of the sand' and face the dangers head on to avoid the risk of them worsening.

Parrot

Parrots are known for being colourful, noisy and imitative: in dreams they may represent someone you find superficial.

In your dream: Ask yourself who the parrot may have represented. An annoying colleague or family member? Or perhaps even yourself?

Vulture

Vultures are associated with death because they feed on carrion – circling vultures over a desert will indicate the location of a recent death or kill.

In your dream: Were they circling overhead? Are you their victim? Do you know who they represent – work colleagues, for example, spreading rumours about you behind your back with an aim to making your work life difficult or impossible to bear? Perhaps this is how you view the family arguing about a will or some other financially based matter. Or are you the vulture, waiting for a moment to swoop in and grab what you can?
(See also Evisceration, page 167)

CREEPERS AND CRAWLERS

Snake

The snake is a very ancient and complex symbol, appearing in almost all cultures and mythologies. It is seen as kundalini, the 'serpent energy' that coils up the spine; as the serpents twining the staff of Asclepius, the Greek god of healing; as Quetzalcoatl, the feathered serpent of the Aztecs; as Niddhogg, the serpent that gnaws at the roots of the world tree Yggdrasil in Norse myth; and as the tempter snake in the biblical garden of Eden. It represents both the positive and negative in one creature, and can be perceived as a symbol of healing, of female power, of authority, destruction, sex or evil.

While it's sensible to treat them with caution, many people fear the **idea** of snakes rather than their physical body: the fact that they can move so swiftly, without legs, over any surface and rear up with just their body as support. The lidless eyes and the flickering tongue make snakes appear somehow eerie.

One special serpentine symbol is the **ouroborous**, the snake swallowing its own tail. It represents either the cycles of life – birth, death, renewal – and all things in balance, or self-destructive behaviour.

In your dream: The snake is a significant image, and it's important to note the other details of the dream. Was it day or night? Were you afraid, curious, nervous or intrigued? Was the snake threatening, ignoring you, or trying to show you something? Was anyone else there? What were the surroundings?

What did the snake represent? Temptation? Sex? Your own sexual power? A healing influence? An animal totem? All of these? Depending on your answers, the snake may suggest

you are more open about your needs and desires with your partner, or more controlled. Or that you stop depending on others and develop your own self-reliance. Is someone you know being a 'snake in the grass' or 'speaking with a forked tongue', working to make your life difficult? Is your subconscious warning you to 'slither away' before disaster strikes? If the snake represents yourself, are you being self-destructive, or revelling in your own power?

Lizard

Varying in size from the tiny skink to the huge monitor, lizards are renowned for their tenacity, their sensitivity to temperature, and the ability to discard, and later regrow, their tails as a defence measure to fool an attacker.

In your dream: Who does the lizard symbolize in the dream? Someone slightly alarming whom you have to care for? A tough, enduring character you grudgingly admire? Or does it represent yourself? What was it doing, and what does that tell you about yourself?

Dinosaur

Just like today's reptiles, dinosaurs came in many shapes and sizes, but we most immediately think of the huge varieties that once walked the earth, whether gentle and ponderous like Diplodocus or an awesome terror like T. rex.

In your dream: What was it about the dinosaur that most impressed you? Its size? Its docility or ferocity? What sparked the dream – have you recently seen a dinosaur film and been inspired by the notion of creatures that big once existing? Or is it a more fundamental interest in evolution and the history of the planet?

Alternatively, do you feel yourself to be a 'dinosaur', out of date and out of touch with the modern world? Does the dream reveal any way you can bring yourself up to date?

Tortoise

These rather endearing creatures stand in our minds as symbols of plodding slowness (sometimes twinned with great determination) and longevity. Retracting its head and legs into its horny shell renders a tortoise safe but immobile, and also acts as a form of camouflage.

In your dream: Are you spending too much time 'in your shell', refusing to face the outside world? Do you feel the need to don 'armour' before leaving the house – make-up, particular clothes or jewellery? Or are you simply feeling old and left behind but trying not to accept it?

Chameleon

What chameleons are best known for is changing their skin colour to blend in with their surroundings.

In your dream: Do you camouflage yourself like the chameleon – or wish you could? A chameleon's eyes can move independently through 180 degrees, giving it superb all-round vision: do you sometimes wish you had 'eyes in the back of your head' like this?

Frog, toad

The tale of the frog turning into a handsome prince when kissed by the beautiful princess is an admonition not to judge by appearances, nor denigrate what seems ugly and unpleasant at first sight.

In your dream: Dreaming of frogs or toads may be a warning from your subconscious to be more aware of the potential opportunities around you, ways of 'leap-frogging' into a career or post you want, even though they may at first seem unpalatable or off-putting.

Scorpion

The scorpion is renowned for the sting in its tail: the Zodiac sign of Scorpio is reputed to have an understanding of the dark side of humanity (see The Shadow, page 148).

In your dream: Who in waking life do you think the scorpion represents? If it's you, are you perhaps being your own worst enemy, driving others away with jealousy or spite? Or is the dream advising you to come to terms with your own inner darkness, the unpleasant things you dislike about yourself?

Spider

The fear of spiders is a very common phobia – a mostly inexplicable one, given the relative sizes of us and them. Some have a very nasty bite, of course, but generally speaking they only attack humans if disturbed. As most spiders are of such insignificant size, it is only for arachnophobes that dream spiders may appear as huge, ferocious creatures.

In your dream: Who do you think the spider represents? A mother or mother-in-law? A grasping, voracious partner, boss or workmate? Someone who has you caught in their web and is preparing to suck the life from you?

Dreaming of being caught in a **spider's web** usually indicates a sense of entrapment in waking life. You may be stuck in a situation where you're sure something bad is inevitable, but you can't escape. Fear, helplessness and a sense of doom predominate, and can easily cross over into waking life. Is there anything you can do to forestall the coming disaster?

Slug, snail

Slow moving, slimy and destructive, these creatures are generally loathed: in dreams they often represent someone or something nasty but not dangerous.

In your dream: Are you feeling 'sluggish' in waking life, with little energy? Do you seem to be moving at a snail's pace? Your subconscious may be suggesting you get your health checked. Alternatively, you may be telling yourself to speed up, find some enthusiasm and participate more fully, rather than dawdling and using the fruit of others' labours.

Ant

In the classic fable, the ant worked hard all summer while the grasshopper sang and danced and had no thought for how he would survive the winter. Ants are an amazing example of cooperative working and living, never stopping their work for the greater good of the colony.

In your dream: Do you resemble the 'industrious ant'? Or do you feel insignificant, just part of a larger whole, as the ant is just one small part of the nest?

Fly

Flies are annoying, disease-carrying pests; our reaction is to swat them if we can.

In your dream: Flies in a dream can mean something small is niggling you, generally unimportant but of personal significance. Alternatively, do you wish you were 'a fly on the wall' somewhere, watching and listening to people's secrets?

Wasp

Wasps are bad-tempered pests, and can spoil otherwise perfect days.

In your dream: Who in your life does the wasp represent? Who is behaving like a wasp, buzzing threateningly and stinging anyone who crosses it, then coming back to sting again – spreading rumours, treating you nastily? Is there any way you can, metaphorically, swat them?

Bee

Traditionally, bees have always been regarded with respect, as much for the sweet honey they create as for their reputation as hard workers. To ensure good fortune, it was important to 'tell the bees' of any family news, of births, marriages or deaths.

In your dream: Are you being a 'busy bee' at work or at home? If the bee was resting, are you working too hard and in need of a break? Or do you act like 'the queen bee', expecting others to do everything for you?

Or might the bees refer to news? Have you recently had good news about your own family?

Moth

Moths can be pests, reducing valuable fabrics to rags – but they can also be very beautiful. The fact that they fly at night makes them slightly mysterious.

In your dream: Who or what did the moth represent? A shadowy figure who comes and goes with no advance warning? A destructive influence, unseen but eating away at the fabric of your life?

A dream of a butterfly or moth **emerging from a cocoon** is a beautiful symbol of renewal and metamorphosis. Are you considering a major change of lifestyle or life path? Such a dream is usually subconscious approval that you have made the right decision.

Butterfly

Butterflies, the 'winged jewels' of the insect world, are beautiful but tragic, their short lives a symbol of how quickly beauty can fade or die.

In your dream: Butterflies in a dream suggest you take time to enjoy life's good things while you have them.

SEA CREATURES

Dolphin

Intelligent, curious, co-operative, the dolphin's relationship with the human race has always been benevolent – and forgiving, on the part of the dolphin, given how many have died as a result of human irresponsibility and greed.

In your dream: The dolphin can play several roles in dreams. Was it a guide, leading you through confusion and doubt to tranquillity and deeper self-awareness? Was it helping you to clarify your emotions? Or did it represent the playful side of yourself striving for expression and release?

Whale

Huge, slow-moving whales are gentle creatures, intelligent and long-lived, although their size has led people to perceive them as monstrous in the past – the blue whale is the largest creature currently living on the planet.

In your dream: Dreaming of whales may indicate something big and very significant happening in your life, probably life-changing and most likely concerning your emotional or spiritual side.

Fish

Dreaming of fish in general suggests a need to relax – your subconscious is providing you with a mental aquarium, proven to be soothing in stressful situations – although if you dream of being *in* an aquarium (or goldfish bowl), you may feel exposed and under scrutiny all the time.

In your dream: The type of fish usually has a bearing on the dream. Are you or those around you being 'slippery as an eel' in your business dealings? Do goldfish remind you of your childhood, or the Japanese tradition that they're baby dragons? Salmon are reputed to grant wisdom in Celtic mythology – do you need advice at the moment?
(See also Symbolic Fish, page 355)

Octopus

Octopuses are remarkably intelligent, but it is their multiple, ultra-mobile tentacles that are most likely to be the prominent feature in a dream.

In your dream: Do you wish you had 'more than one pair of hands'? Are you trying to do too much? Are too many people trying to 'grab your attention', 'throttling' you? Or perhaps the menace is more physical – do your work colleagues have 'wandering hands'?

Shark

Sharks are cold-blooded, ruthless predators. In dreams, they generally represent people circling, closing in for a kill.

In your dream: Do you feel under threat that someone is waiting to 'take a bite' out of you? Does the dream show any way out?

Starfish

Starfish are renowned for being able to regrow missing limbs; some varieties can even grow a whole new starfish from a lost limb. The starfish is a symbol of regeneration and perpetuation, a sign that life continues despite adverse circumstances.

In your dream: Starfish represent hope, a subconscious awareness that matters are improving.

Crab

Crabs move erratically from side to side. One of the characteristics of the Zodiac sign of Cancer the Crab is that of a hoarder, finding it difficult to throw anything away as it 'might come in handy later'.

In your dream: Is the crab in the dream advising you to clear the clutter, or warning you not to get rid of something important? Are you trying to evade someone, or are they trying to evade you?

[See also Water, page 63; Sea, page 29]

3 HUMANS

Our bodies, senses and emotions are integral to our being, and dreams that focus on them can alert us to areas of our physical or emotional lives that need attention. Also included here are some themes that seem to be universal, common throughout time and to all cultures. The chapter ends with a few archetypes, original patterns after which other things are modelled. Carl Jung organized the concept of archetypes into psychological constructs, but the concept had been in existence for far longer, possibly since the beginning of conscious thought.

THE HUMAN BODY

Body parts can also carry sexual symbolism – there's a school of thought that associates any long, cylindrical item with a phallus, any bowl- or hill-shaped image with a breast, and a hole in anything with the vagina . Sometimes the correlation is obvious, but it's not wise to think that every single instance of such symbols relates to sex.

Head

We experience much of the world via our heads – eyes for sight, nose for smell, tongue for taste, ears for hearing. The head also contains our brain, the complex organ with which we make sense of the world. The importance we attach to the head is clear in modern parlance: rulers are referred to as 'heads of state' and the 'head' of anything, from head of the family to head boy, is top in an institution.

In your dream: What were the circumstances in the dream? Was the head someone you know: a mother, father or authority figure? Seeing only the back of the head suggests estrangement, unfamiliarity or an impersonal perception of the person – perhaps they are too 'high' for you to have any real feeling of connection.

A **disembodied head** – a somewhat horrific image – suggests you feel disorientated, able to think but not to act effectively. Was the head your own, in which case are you trying to do too much by yourself without the necessary support of others? If someone else's, do you see that person as superior yet ineffectual – like an incompetent boss?

Face

We recognize others by their faces, and can usually do so from a considerable distance. Our faces are unique and very personal, the image we present to the world.

In your dream: Whose face was it? Your own or someone else's? Familiar or a stranger? A happy dream of the face of someone you haven't seen for a while may be prompting you to contact them – or letting you know that they will be in contact themselves soon.

Meeting strangers may be warning you to be more reserved in your dealings with others, especially if the dream was at all threatening. Is someone you know being 'two-faced', pleasant to your face but trying to harm you behind your back?

Your own face disfigured can indicate low self-esteem, especially if others react with revulsion; alternatively it may suggest that beauty is only skin deep and you fear others finding the inner you to be ugly.
(See also Stranger, page 142)

Eyes

To have people watching you intently is as disturbing in a dream as it can be in waking life. A dream in which eyes feature prominently may simply be telling you to 'use your eyes', observe, pay attention to others, to your environment.

In your waking life: Are you being accused of something, rightly or wrongly? Is your behaviour under scrutiny, at work or elsewhere? Or are you deliberately blinding yourself to what's going on around you? Remember the old adage 'there's none so blind as those who will not see'.
(See also Sight, page 126)

Mouth

Mouths have three main functions: to express our thoughts in speech, to eat and to kiss (which may be considered a form of communication).

In your dream: Who was **speaking**, and was it to greet, offer advice, complain, argue? Was the setting pleasant or hostile? Were you comfortable, aggressive or fearful? Do you have to 'have words' with someone and are dreading it? Or looking forward to telling someone how you feel?

If the dream focused on **eating**, was it fastidious, small bites, chewing before swallowing, or uncouth, tearing and swallowing as though starving? The former may indicate a concern for appearance over reality, of needing to keep tight control over behaviour, while the latter suggests a need for sustenance, and not necessarily just food. Communication and the expression of affection are also functions of the mouth, after all.

Kissing is a very intimate activity, from the gentle kiss a parent gives a child to the passionate kiss between lovers. To enjoy kissing in a dream indicates a healthy acceptance of yourself and your own sexuality, although if it's illicit – the other person being a friend's lover or spouse, for example – it would be best to consider the dream a pleasant private fantasy rather than trying to act it out!

Tongue

Vital for tasting our food as well as for clear speech, the tongue is an expressive organ, stuck out between the lips to express disrespect, 'tongue-tied' in the presence of someone who alarms or overwhelms us, 'tongue-in-cheek' when teasing or joking.

In your dream: Are you delivering or receiving a well-deserved 'tongue lashing'? Or in your waking life is someone 'speaking with forked tongue', spreading lies and rumours about you – or are you doing so to another person? (See also Taste, page 127)

Teeth

Healthy teeth make eating a pleasure, and contribute to our overall attractiveness, especially when we smile. Rotten, misshapen or missing teeth reveal a lack of personal care and hygiene.

In your dream: Teeth may indicate that the speech that comes out of that mouth shouldn't be trusted. **Teeth bared behind full lips** may represent the fear or threat of emasculation.

Nose

A large nose indicating its owner also has a large penis is a persistent myth, more likely to be wishful thinking than anything else!

In your dream: Dreams in which noses feature prominently may simply be advising you not to be 'nosy', or to let others interfere in your own affairs.
(See also Smell, page 129)

Ears

A dream where normal ears are prominent is most usually a warning to listen to what's being said by others, advice to pay attention.

In your dream: Were the ears unusual in some way – pointed and elf-like, for example? This may indicate a wish for something different, exotic or fantastic in your life.
(See also Hearing, page 126)

Neck

The neck supports the head: we would be vulnerable to attack without its flexibility and strength, which allow us to look easily in all directions without having to turn our body.

In your dream: Are you or someone you know being 'stiff-necked', stubborn and uncooperative? Or are you being advised not to 'stick your neck out', to be inconspicuous and keep your head down?

Hair

Hair is often the 'crowning beauty', especially for women, and a full head of hair is traditionally a sign of virility for men – hence the anxiety associated with baldness.

In your dream: Hair in dreams usually indicates your perception of yourself and your attractiveness to others. Rich, shining hair symbolizes confidence, lank, uncared-for locks a lack of self-esteem. A dream of **going bald** may suggest that you feel you're losing control of your life. [See also Hairdresser, page 178]

Shoulders

Broad shoulders are associated with strength, and bowed shoulders with fear, depression or submission.

In your dream: Were you weighed down in the dream, as though carrying the 'weight of the world on your shoulders'? Or were you 'turning a cold shoulder' to someone? If the former, your subconscious may be warning you to find a way of easing the stresses of your waking life. If the latter, do you feel uneasy in their company? Can you pinpoint why?

Hands

The human hand, in combination with the reasoning brain, has been responsible for the development of human civilization. Our flexible, adept hands with their opposable thumbs are capable of both creation and destruction.

In your dream: Were they your own hands or another's? Were you taking 'your life in your hands' – for good or ill – or 'handing over' control to another? Or was it 'the hand of fate' guiding (or meddling in) your life?

Were the hands using tools, performing useful activities, creating something? Or were they being used to destroy or injure? How did you feel about their actions? Remember, sometimes it's necessary to tear down the old and damaged in order to make space for the new and better.

Arms

Humans use their arms for balance, for reaching and holding, cuddling and restraining.

In your dream: A dream prominently featuring arms may indicate that you feel yourself the victim of someone else's 'strong-arm' tactics. Or that you're missing someone or something to hold: dreaming of your arms being empty is not uncommon after a bereavement, the end of a relationship or a child leaving home.

Fingers

As well as enabling us to do many tasks, fingers point out directions, beckon and bear rings that may be significant.

In your dream: Are you being pointed in a particular direction? Or is someone singling you out, for blame or praise? Is the dream telling you to 'pull your finger out' and get a move on with work or a home project? A dream focusing on your ring finger may indicate a wish for a permanent romantic or emotional relationship – or an end to your current one if a ring that had been there is missing. (See also Ring, page 295)

Chest, breast

Dreaming of a woman's breasts is most likely simply erotic, although the dream could indicate a longing for maternal care, either giving or receiving.

A dream that focuses on a man's chest may be erotic, although it's most likely indicative of a yearning for someone strong on whom to rely, especially if you're having persistent problems in waking life.

In your dream: Was the dream sexual or was it accompanied by a feeling or yearning to be nurtured and look after? Full breasts may also suggest that their owner will be able to breastfeed well, which in itself is suggestive of the act that creates a baby.
(See also Mother, page 136)

Stomach, abdomen

The stomach is associated with food and digestion, but also tolerance, satisfaction and illness.

In your waking life: Are you having trouble 'stomaching' certain people or events? Or are you having physical problems with your digestive system? If it's bothering you enough that it's reflected in your dreams, it may be sensible to take action in your waking life.

Groin

A dream of someone's groin, male or female, generally indicates a healthy interest in sex, and perhaps in comparing sexual experiences with another. A more interesting dream is finding yourself equipped with the genitals of the opposite sex.

In your dream: Are you intrigued as to how it would feel to be the other gender? Over and above the fear or anguish this may initially cause, consider why you might have dreamed it. Do you unconsciously wish that you were a member of the opposite sex? What did the rest of your body look like in the dream? How did others react to you, and you to them?

Back

The back symbolizes willpower and determination: it supports the whole body and allows us to stand upright.

In your dream: Is your subconscious encouraging you to 'put your back into' a project? Or perhaps warning you that sometimes bending prevents breaking: are you being too stubborn regarding a particular matter or person?

Buttocks

An obvious sexual connotation. To some, buttocks, especially if well-rounded, may suggest breasts. The fact they are close to the genitals may also make them an object of arousal. But to admire them requires the owner to be facing away from you, so that you cannot see their face, which has the effect of depersonalising their sexual appeal: they become more an object of gratification.

Alternatively, buttocks can simply denote 'backside'.

In your dream: If buttocks are a recurrent feature in a sexual dream, do you prefer impersonal sex, or sex with strangers. Or perhaps you simply prefer not to let your partner see your reactions, your emotions, while you are with them?

Or, in your waking life, are you spending too much time sitting on your rear, letting life pass you by? Or is your subconscious suggesting someone – you, perhaps – needs a kick up the backside?

Legs

Before Homo sapiens developed other methods of transport, our legs were our only means to move from place to place, and even with today's more sedentary lifestyle their function remains the same. A dream focusing on legs may have sexual connotations but is more likely your subconscious stressing the need for action – finding a way to escape an unpleasant or hostile situation.

In your dream: Did your dream involve an urge to be on the move, or was it primarily sexual? Many people find long legs attractive – whether because they make the individual appear taller or because they are linked with the notion of health and litheness and hence sexual stamina, is up to you to decide.

Internal organs

With the exception of the heart (see page 124), dreams featuring internal organs aren't common, except in nightmares (see pages 166–168).

In your dream: If a particular organ makes an appearance, it might be sensible to pay attention to how you're treating it in your waking life: you may tell yourself you aren't doing any harm but your subconscious knows better. If you're a smoker, for example, dreaming of unhealthy **lungs** may be warning you of the damage you are doing; for a heavy drinker, a dream of ailing **kidneys** or **liver** suggests the same.

Feet

If our head represents our ability to reason, to imagine and make real what we envisage, our feet symbolize the opposite – being firmly grounded in the physical world.

In your waking life: Are you 'standing on your own two feet' or are you overly reliant on others?

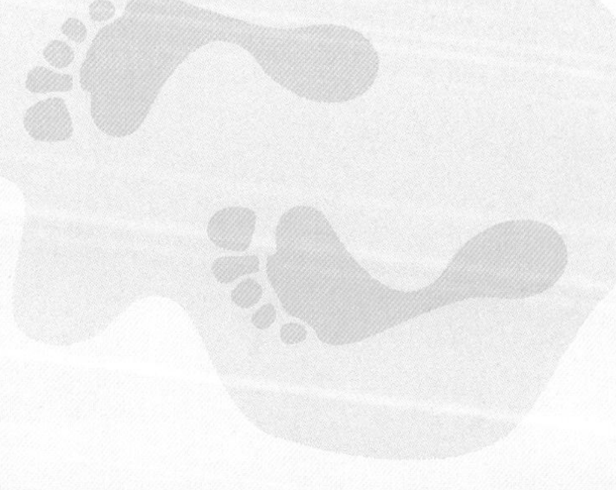

Skin

Skin forms a protective barrier around our bodies, keeping infection out and our bodily processes in. A focus on skin, your own or other people's, in dreams can have a variety of meanings. It may be taken literally, as a health warning or aspect of beauty, or denote a condition, such as being 'thin-skinned' – overly sensitive to criticism – or thick-skinned', blundering through life, oblivious to the feelings or sensitivities of others.

In your dream: Were you or somebody else 'thin-skinned' or 'thick-skinned'. Did you feel like 'brothers/sisters under the skin' with others? Or is your subconscious warning you that 'beauty is only skin deep'?

A dream of **diseased or damaged skin** may indicate that you feel your personal protection is compromised, whether through physical illness or more generally, in your work or at home. Consider the cause, and if you have any health concerns, as always seek medical advice.
(See also Nakedness, page 144)

Heart

The heart is the one organ that does commonly appear in dreams – at least, the popular heart shape that has become synonymous with expressions of love, and something so fundamental in our lives is bound to be reflected in our dreams. Its symbolism in dreams is fairly straightforward.

In your dream: A bright, whole and healthy red or pink heart indicates happiness in and with your love life. A broken, pale or miscoloured heart shape suggest the opposite. Have you 'given your heart' to someone, or has someone 'broken your heart' in your waking life?

Blood

Blood is a powerful image. Its colour symbolizes passion and danger, and it is vital to life. A variety of blood-related sayings all reflect its importance: 'blood brothers' are closer than siblings, while 'blood ties' and 'blood is thicker than water' indicate the strength of family bonds. Sexually it can relate to the tearing of the hymen when a virgin is 'deflowered', once seen as proof of the male's virility.

In your dream: Most people find the idea of bleeding instinctively troubling, since blood is so essential to life. Actually **liking** the sight, smell or taste of blood might indicate a worrying psychological condition. Alternatively, especially if the dream involves vampires or ghouls, it may simply be a form of role-play.

Making a lover bleed may symbolize having control over that person, but is not an overly healthy image.

Bleeding from a particular limb or organ may indicate either something physically wrong or a symbolic loss of its function (see also specific body parts in this chapter). **Bleeding hands** may suggest a subconscious feeling of having 'blood on your hands' – deliberately harming another person's reputation or life.

(See also Red page 256; Vampire, page 371; Stigmata, page 352)

Menstrual blood

The onset of menstruation symbolizes the young woman's ability to bear children.

In your dream: Menstrual blood may indicate relief, if you feared you might be pregnant, or distress if the reverse is true. It can also suggest embarrassment in sexual matters.

SENSES

Many people find that they can't smell or taste anything in a dream, but dreams focusing on one sense to the exclusion of the others indicate a need to bring that sense into play in waking life.

Sight

We may not be aware of it, but everything we see, even subliminally, is stored away in our subconscious.

In your waking life: Are you 'turning a blind eye' when you should be paying attention? Trying not to see what's right in front of you because it's too painful, embarrassing or annoying for you to willingly scrutinize? Or are you too self-absorbed to be aware of what's happening around you?

A dream in which you can see, but not speak, might indicate that you need to take a back seat for a while, take time to observe rather than be involved.

(See also Eyes, page 113)

Hearing

Voices in a dream, or a background noise or soundtrack can throw light on to the interpretation of a dream.

In your dream: Can you hear what's being said? Or is it being whispered just out of your hearing? Are you listening to what other people say in your waking life, or do you only half-hear what's being said? Are people talking about you behind your back?

A dream of someone crying or pleading for help may indicate a subconscious awareness of a friend or colleague in trouble. Is there some way you could assist them?

(See also Ears, page 116)

Touch

A focus on the sense of touch suggests that you may be 'out of touch' with the feelings of those around you, or maybe your own, especially if you can't see or hear anything.

In your dream: Were you deprived of your other senses? This is likely to be a way of emphasizing the need to 'be in touch'. A dream where what you are touching is soft and luxurious may be erotic and sensuous and suggest your sensual nature rather than having any deeper meaning!

Taste

Being able to taste in a dream may be nothing more than a reflection of the pleasure you gain from tasting – food, drink, your partner's skin – in your waking life. If you're eating a particular food, it may indicate you are lacking something provided by that foodstuff. It might be wise to check its main constituents, whether it contains specific elements that are lacking in your diet. Remember, your subconscious absorbs information that you may not be consciously aware of taking in!

In your dream: What were you eating? Were you enjoying it or was the taste horrible?
(See also Food and Drink, pages 261–282)

Temperature

Not one of the recognized five physical senses, but nevertheless something we feel intimately.

In your dream: As long as there's no physical reason, such as a cold wind through the window or the heating set too high, feeling 'hot' may simply be one element of an erotic dream, or suggest that you feel restrained in your waking life, smouldering unseen, and are finding release in your dreams. Similarly, feeling cold may express a fear that others see you as cold, unfeeling or frigid.

Pressure

Not a commonly recognized sense, but anyone who has felt the approach of a thunderstorm like a hand pressing down on their neck or the top of their head, with associated headaches and irritability, will understand that it should be viewed as a sense!

In your dream: If there's no physical, barometric reason for the sensation, it may indicate that you feel 'under pressure' to succeed at work or in a relationship. Alternatively, do you need to 'let off steam', as though releasing the pressure in a pressure-cooker?

Smell

Scent in dreams is often influenced by the aroma in the room with you while you sleep – having a fragrance you like on a tissue beside the bed may help your dreams to be pleasant. If, however, the smell is unpleasant and there's no physical reason for it, consider what it means to you in waking life. Do you associate the smell of the sewer with less savoury elements of yourself or those around you? We use the phrases 'mind like a sewer' and 'get your mind out of the gutter' to joke about these perfectly normal aspects of life, but many people prefer to keep them hidden.

In your dream: What were you smelling? The sweet natural fragrance of flowers? A manufactured perfume? Food or drink, such as coffee, bread, chocolate or fish? The rich earthy smell of a wood or the fresh, invigorating scent of a sea breeze? Pine or cut grass? Bleach or rotting vegetables? Incense or the stink of blocked drains?

EMOTIONS

The emotional 'flavour' of a dream has a significant bearing on its overall meaning. No matter how pleasant the trappings, if it's accompanied by a feeling of unease or fear, your subconscious is warning you that all is not as it seems. They tend to reflect our deepest fears or simple unadulterated joys, situations over which we have no control.

Love

The word 'love' encompasses an enormous spectrum and many degrees of emotion.

In your dream: To whom or what is the love directed? Your partner, child, family? This suggests a happy, healthy relationship with those close to you. If it's to someone you know only by sight, or a stranger, perhaps you are subconsciously yearning for variety or excitement in your life. However, if it's towards a celebrity, the dream is more likely to be simply a pleasant fantasy.
(See also Other People, pages 135–142)

Hate

Hatred is a dangerous and ugly emotion, one we would probably rather not acknowledge, but it is also a part of life and ignoring it only makes it worse. It needs to be addressed and managed properly to avoid deep and lasting harm. Dreaming is one way in which our minds cope, acting out our loathing mentally rather than inflicting it on others.

In your dream: What was the object of your hatred in the dream? If a person, is there any way you can come to terms with why you loathe them so much? If a situation, can you escape from it?

Greed

Greed is rooted in insecurity or feelings of inferiority, a desire to own more or to have what others possess, to boost a lack of self-worth – making up in material possessions for what you feel you lack in personal merit.

In your dream: How was greed represented? Was it simply a feeling or were you hoarding objects, overeating, stopping someone else from acquiring what they wanted? If physical possessions were involved, what were they?
(See also Jealousy, Envy, page 133)

Fear

Dreams can reveal the source of our fears, but not always in a straightforward way. If a person or situation frightened you in a dream, ask yourself why. What do they represent in waking life? The post, for example, might be feared because it brings unwelcome news, or a flock of birds may represent flight and worry about a forthcoming journey, or possibly someone close 'taking flight' or 'leaving the nest' and striking out on their own.

In your dream: Was there a definable source of the fear? Can you work out what it might represent when you equate it to events or expectations in your waking life?

Pride, vanity

While pride can be a positive quality if it's justified, it can rapidly turn to arrogance if it's misplaced. Vanity is never an attractive quality, and to dream of being called vain indicates a self-centredness that may be impeding your progress, either in your work or love life.

In your dream: What were you proud of? Friends or family? Your accomplishments or work? Or more trivial things – your looks, your clothes, the way you speak? Was the dream trying to warn you that 'pride comes before a fall'?

Sorrow

Feeling deeply unhappy or grief-stricken is distressing enough in waking life; when it appears in dreams it can be even worse. The feeling is usually associated with an actual event – bereavement, divorce, other sudden and unexpected loss, for example – and understandable in those terms.

In your dream: If you feel miserable in a dream without obvious cause, is there something you're refusing to acknowledge?

Boredom

Boredom is usually the sign of either an unused, lazy mind or of a particularly brilliant one without sufficient challenges, in dreams as well as in waking life. To be bored in a dream suggests you need to take a close look at your life, your working environment and social circle, and see where they can be made more challenging and interesting. A dream of being boring to other people suggests you suspect that you are not an interesting person in your waking life.

In your dream: Is the dream an accurate reflection, or just a haunting fear? The latter may indicate an underlying insecurity, especially if the dream is recurring.

Jealousy, envy

Jealousy and envy are unpleasant emotions. In dreams they may appear as spiteful behaviour or language, being ignored, having something stolen, or being attacked.

Envy is closely related to jealousy, but is less personal: where a person may be jealous of a friend's good looks or charm, they may envy the rich their wealth, or the famous their celebrity status. In dreams, what the dreamer envies may indicate something they fiercely want to possess.

In your dream: If you feel jealous in a dream for no obvious reason, consider the situation in your waking life. Are you jealous of someone, or is someone jealous of you? Is the jealousy directed at a person, a possession, or something less tangible, like a good reputation? What form does this take in the dream? Jealousy is often described as being poisonous: are you **being poisoned** in the dream? Does the dream indicate anything you can do to alleviate the situation?

Hopelessness

The feeling of being swept along by forces outside of your control is perhaps more prevalent in dreams than in real life, simply because, unless you've learned how to do so, you have no conscious control, no way to direct the dream. A distinct feeling of hopelessness in a dream suggests you feel the same in waking life.

In your waking life: Are you stuck in a situation from which you can see no escape? Is there anything in the dream that indicates a way you can extricate yourself?

Joy

Feeling joy in a dream usually reflects the state of something in your waking life.

In your dream: If you aren't consciously aware of being particularly happy, consider what causes you such joy in the dream, then think about why that person, object, situation or idea makes you so happy. Is there any way you can duplicate this in waking life?

OTHER PEOPLE

Partner

It's not surprising that the person who most closely shares your life often appears in your dreams or, if you don't have a partner in waking life, that your dreams provide you with one. We all need someone with whom to share some part of our life. Ideally the relationship is one of love, cooperation, consideration and trust, but of course very few relationships are ideal!

An interesting feature of dreams is that a partner's form is often quite different from their appearance in waking life, yet you always know who they are. It's worth noting how they look: this can indicate how you perceive and react to them mentally – an older and apparently staid partner may appear young and dynamic, for example, if you feel them to be young at heart.

In your dream: Does the dream point out aspects of your partner that you find unpleasant or that you've been deliberately ignoring? Consider what you were both doing in the dream: were you fighting, was one of you walking away or were you talking face to face? What does this indicate about the best way to improve matters?

A dream of leaving or changing partners may suggest you're unsatisfied with your current situation, and may need to take steps to resolve issues between you.

Mother

Mother as a concept symbolizes security, nourishment, fertility and unconditional love, but may also involve the negative qualities of destruction, possessiveness, malevolent secrecy and poisonous competition. For most of us, our first and arguably most important relationship is with our mother. Her behaviour and attitude towards us can colour our relationships with others all through our lives. Which aspect you dream about depends to a large extent on your relationship with your mother.

In your dream: Who does the mother figure represent – mother, boss, carer or even yourself? Mother as an archetype may be an unspoken wish for sanctuary if you feel unloved or abandoned. A dream of your own mother, however, may be more complex. Do you admire her? Are there elements of her character you dislike? Do you share any of these traits? Was the dream one of trying to escape an overbearing or repressive mother or were you trying to express her good qualities in your own life?

Father

Father as a concept symbolizes protector and judge in its positive aspect, or the arrogant, domineering head of the family in its negative. As with the mother, the father figure in your dream will depend on your waking life relationship,

In your dream: Dreaming of a father figure may indicate a wish to relinquish responsibility for your troubles for a while, to rest and recover. As with the mother image, your relationship with your own father will colour any dream in which he appears.

Child

The image of the child symbolizes both innocence and optimism, and the selfish, tantrum-throwing brat. Generally, dream children symbolize optimism, hope for the future, innocence and playfulness.

In your dream: Does the child represent yourself, your own children or children you know, or someone who persists in acting like a child? Are you in touch with your 'inner child', or are you depending too much on others, acting like a child and denying your responsibilities? What was the child trying to teach you? To enjoy life? To worry less?

Sibling

Brothers and sisters, if you have them, can appear as themselves in dreams, or your mind may conjure up dream-siblings, whether or not you have any in your waking life.

In your dream: If you have siblings, the dream may indicate areas where your relationship needs attention. Were you arguing, and if so, about what?

If you don't have siblings, is the dream suggesting that you consider other people to be brothers and sisters – do you have a sense of brotherhood with a particular group or party? Have you always wanted siblings – in which case the dream may simply be wishful thinking, an idealized view of what it would be like to have a brother or sister.

Friends

Dreaming of friends is often no more than a reflection of your waking life, unless one particular friend is featured strongly. A dream peopled by friends may also be a form of wish-fulfilment if you feel lonely or depressed, or lack trustworthy friends in your waking life.

In your dream: Was a particular friend trying to tell you something? Or would you like them to become more than simply a friend?

If dream-friends were bringing an end to loneliness, did the dream give any indication of how you can improve matters in your waking life? Were you in a particular place where meeting new people is made easy, for example, like a club or evening class?

Colleagues

A dream focusing on colleagues may indicate your feelings towards those you work with. Do you trust them? Are they friends as well as workmates?

In your dream: Is there one in particular with whom you share a special rapport, or about whom you feel uneasy? Does the dream indicate why?

Grandparents

Although the meaning of the image will depend on your feelings about your grandparents, in general in dreams they represent stability and caring. Grandparents can also represent family roots, especially if you have never met them, or if they are deceased.

In your dream: Meeting grandparents can suggest that you feel disconnected from family life. A visit to them may indicate that you feel unloved or burdened in your current relationships and are yearning for something less demanding.

Crowd

A dream of being in a crowd can be exhilarating or terrifying, depending on its purpose.

In your dream: Were you at a concert or public event, having a wonderful time? Was this a memory or wish-fulfilment? Were you at a demonstration, publicly declaring your support for a cause? If you've been too hesitant to do so in waking life, maybe your subconscious is nudging you to take some affirmative action.

Dreaming of being unwillingly caught in a hostile crowd, or having a crowd after you, may reflect what is happening in waking life. Are you being forced to do something against your principles, on threat of public punishment or humiliation? Is there any way you can escape?

Fictional characters

The impact of films and books can be very powerful, and carry over into our dreams.

In your dream: Does the character possess qualities you'd like to own? Or would you like to meet someone like this? [See also Superhero, page 319 and other mythical characters in The Supernatural, pages 368–379]

Neighbours

Most people have neighbours, and most manage to co-exist reasonably happily together. Dissent in a dream, however, may indicate an underlying problem – an argument over noise levels, toys left where they may be tripped over, an unacceptably overgrown or unkempt garden?

In your dream: Did the dream reveal any way to resolve a problem with neighbours in your waking life? Coming to blows might have been very satisfying and no doubt cathartic, but it would probably not be a good idea!

Alternatively, were you trying to keep up with your neighbours but were frustrated because they always had more and better than you? Such a dream may indicate feelings of inferiority that might be better consciously examined.

Strangers

Many of the characters in dreams are simply background strangers, a reflection of waking life, where we are frequently surrounded by people we don't know and with whom we have no wish to be acquainted. A dream of being threatened by strangers is a different matter, however.

In your dream: Did you feel threatened? Have you experienced a threatening stranger, a mugging, robbery or stalking, for example, in your waking life? If so, you may be still suffering from it and it might be wise to seek counselling.
(See also Being Attacked, page 146)

Celebrities

Dreaming of meeting a celebrity isn't that unusual these days, when so much personal information is available, and is most often nothing more than fantasy fulfilment. Most of us have our favourite actor, singer or writer, and it's very enjoyable to imagine spending time with them, as long as you don't expect the dream to come true!

In your dream: What does the person mean to you? What do they represent? Sex appeal, wealth, fame, adulation? Do you feel that being close to the individual means that some of their attraction might rub off on you?

Alternatively, if you've actually met the person in the dream, it's more likely to be a happy memory. Did you learn anything from the encounter? Some way of dealing with happenings in your waking life?
(See also relevant people in Occupations, page 169 and Entertainment and Sport, page 204)

UNIVERSAL DREAMS

Flying

A dream of flying under your own power is one of the most enjoyable dreams known. To soar above all obstacles, to be free to go where you want, is a sheer joy. It's a dream that tends to be more prevalent in children who have few responsibilities or worries, and the elderly who have effectively left most of their responsibilities and worries behind them, rather than adults, who are usually weighed down by the burdens of life.

In your dream: Dreaming of flying as an adult usually indicates that you are feeling unusually happy, buoyant and optimistic, such dreams generally occur when you've overcome your problems and made real progress in life.

Occasionally a dream of flight is accompanied by feelings of fear or unhappiness. This usually reflects a subconscious wish to 'fly away' from all the problems besetting you in your waking life.

Nakedness

Unconcern at your nakedness suggests you feel free and unencumbered by the conventions of society.

Embarrassment or humiliation may indicate you are heavily influenced by the culture in which you live, perhaps allowing others to dictate what you should and should not do. Dreaming of being naked in public can have several different meanings, depending on your reaction.

In your dream: Were you hugely embarrassed? Maybe you feel inferior to the people around you, because you have revealed too much of yourself, or because you are ashamed of your body? Did you feel resigned to facing up to having all your camouflage stripped away for others to see you as you really are? Or did the dream include an element of relief, that now you have no excuse not to be honest because there's nothing to hide behind?

Running to escape

Running for your life is one of the nastier dreams, often accompanied by feelings of terror.

In your dream: Are you vainly trying to escape from an identifiable person or situation? Does this reflect a situation in your waking life? Do you have any alternative to running away? Might it be better to face the problem and deal with it?

Occasionally such a dream has no obvious cause. It may be that life itself – the state of the world, politics, the economy, things over which you have no direct control – is causing the dream. Unfortunately there's not an awful lot you can do about this except try to find something positive on which to focus, friends, perhaps, or a particular personal skill.

Falling

A fear of falling is perfectly natural – the landing hurts, and can cause injury. In dreams, falling usually represents insecurity of the worse kind, a nausea-invoking feeling of plummeting downwards with nothing to hang on to or to break the fall. It is often accompanied by feelings of panic, hopelessness or depression.

In your dream: Falling is a relatively common dream for those suffering a 'fall in fortunes', including bankruptcy, divorce or the death of someone relied upon or precious. (See also Emotions, page 130)

Performing but unprepared

There are several variations; having to take a test for which you haven't studied, having to give a demonstration on an unfamiliar subject, or being on stage but not knowing your lines. The dream usually occurs at a stressful time, when you feel you are being 'tested' and may be found wanting.

In your dream: If it's a physical test, are you facing some sort of active challenge in waking life? If an exam, is it an intellectual test?

Being lost or trapped

Helplessness and panic are, understandably, common feelings in such a dream, which is usually a straightforward symbol of how you feel in waking life, lost and not knowing how to find your way back on to the path, or trapped in circumstances from which you can't escape.

In your dream: Are there any people or symbols that may help you escape?

Being attacked

It's not surprising that this has been a common dream throughout history. Today the attacker is more likely to be another human, but the fear of attack by a large animal remains in our subconscious.

In your dream: Is your mind reliving the freezing fear and helplessness associated with the attack? Are you vulnerable and defenceless in waking life?

ARCHETYPES

Archetypes in dreams reveal fundamental elements of ourselves, our motivations, needs, desires and what we believe about ourselves.

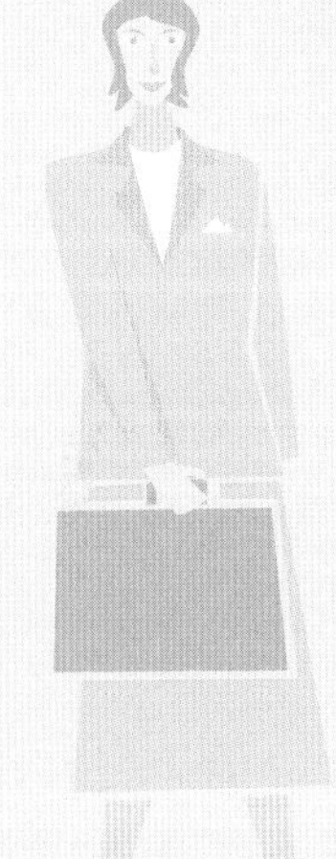

Anima/animus

Everyone contains elements of both the masculine and feminine within them. The aggressive, forceful businesswoman, for example, is perhaps unconsciously tapping into the masculine aspects of her character, while the sensitive, considerate pediatric male nurse is accessing the feminine.

Jung called the feminine side of a male's psyche the anima, while the masculine aspect of a female's psyche is referred to as the animus.

In your dream: The animus usually appears in women's dreams as a handsome young male, strong, assertive, active. His positive aspect embodies the qualities you are lacking or repress: accepting them offers you the opportunity to rebalance yourself. His negative side warns that you may be aggressive, critical and controlling.

The anima generally appears in men's dreams as a lovely young female, open, responsive, creative and often in the guise of a mythical creature like an elf or mermaid. Her positive aspect embodies the qualities of consideration for others, love, trust to instinct. Her negative side may be petulant, whining, easily offended.

Shadow

The shadow is the dark, unpleasant side of ourselves, the part we prefer to hide or repress. If you find yourself acting what you would consider to be out of character in the dream, it may be your shadow trying to teach you a lesson. It's important to acknowledge that the shadow is an integral part of yourself, whether you like it or not.

In your dream: A forceful, assertive shadow possesses qualities that would help you advance in life if you are naturally mild and self-effacing: that assertiveness can be brought to the fore in waking life. A shadow that appears angry and violent in a usually calm, aloof person may be subconscious advice to engage more fully with life, feel more completely rather than simply observing objectively.

Trickster

The trickster attempts to prevent you achieving your goals by putting obstacles in your way. The trickster is a teacher, and no matter how frustrating his/her obstacles seem at the time, the lessons learned are immensely valuable and generally prove to be worthwhile in the end.

In your dream: Are you shown to be deliberately sabotaging your own chances, out of fear of failure (or success, which can be as frightening as failure) or competition, or because you are afraid of the sense of anti-climax, of having 'no new worlds to conquer' after attaining your goal? Or is the trickster telling you that you need to learn patience and persistence? Or maybe the trickster acts to puncture your vanity, make fun of you, to show you aren't the most important person in the world.

Hero

The traditional hero-figure has humble origins, but overcomes adversity through his/her strength, and goes on to fight against and overcome hostile forces, sometimes for personal benefit, often for the benefit of others. Heroes represent the quest for understanding and wisdom.

In your dream: The appearance of a hero usually indicates that you now have the maturity and power to take control of your life – the hero is the part of you that acknowledges your inner strengths and weakness. The negative side of the hero is arrogant, self-deluding and condescending: if this negative image appears in the dream, it might be a good idea to consider your own actions and change them if necessary. (See also Superhero, page 379)

4 THE HUMAN CONDITION

There are certain events that happen to all of us, the obvious being birth and death. In between, however, are a host of situations and phenomena that may not be uniquely human, but which nevertheless affect us all deeply. Suffering loneliness and loss, falling prey to temptations and phobias and encountering violence in one form or another are also all part of the human condition.

Birth

A dream of being born most often accompanies the start of a new phase of your life – a new intimate relationship, a move to a new home, job or country, even the conscious decision to start a family.

In your dream: Was being born a struggle or did it bring a sense of arrival? Is there something happening in your waking life for which the birth dream might be a symbol?

Pregnancy

Your feelings about being pregnant in a dream are usually an accurate reflection of your true, if hidden, feelings in waking life, whether the situation involves an actual pregnancy or is an analogy for something else – a long-term plan, for example.

In your dream: What emotions accompanied the pregnancy? Joy because the baby was wanted, fear in case something was wrong? Desperation because the baby was unplanned, the result of rape or disabled in some way?

Giving birth

If you are actually pregnant, dreaming of giving birth may be a kind of mental rehearsal for the actual event. If you aren't expecting, or if you're male, the dream most likely refers to a new project, at home or at work, which is about to start.

In your dream: Did you find the birth easy or difficult? If the birth was easy, you feel confident that all will proceed smoothly. Conversely, if it was a prolonged and painful labour, you are probably rightly anticipating difficulties and animosity.

Sex

Sex is a fundamental human drive, geared to perpetuate the species. It's also intended to be a highly enjoyable activity, although some institutions and some religions present it as shameful in order to control their adherents.

You may dream of violent sex, rape or torture, if you have had bad sexual experiences in the past, find sex painful, or are afraid of the vulnerability involved. Sex can also be used as a threat or punishment, a way to humiliate.

In your dream: If your dream was pleasant, simply accept it for what it was, a sign of a healthy attitude towards sex. If violence or threat was involved, do you know why? Are you reacting to a threatening atmosphere in waking life; are you being sexually harassed, for example, and dreaming of 'turning the tables' on the perpetrator?

Any dream involving violent, painful sex, especially if the dream is a recurrent one, might indicate a need to seek professional help.

Partnership

Having someone to rely on in adult life – a close friend, lover or colleague – is of great importance to our mental health. Mutual trust and cooperation, respect, affection, even love, add immeasurably to the quality of our life. A dream featuring your partner or partnership, stresses the importance of the relationship.

In your dream: What was your partner doing? What were you doing? Was there anything to indicate that things aren't as they should be? That your partner might be betraying you? That you haven't shown them how much you appreciate their support, or vice versa?

Illness

If you are generally in good health, a dream of suffering from a particular illness, especially if the dream recurs, is best taken seriously: the subconscious is often more aware of what's happening within your body, while your conscious mind tends to 'tune out' anything it doesn't want to hear. Worry about the actual illness of a member of your family may cause you to dream of developing the same ailment, especially if it is a hereditary one.

If the illness isn't physiological, consider the alternative meanings. Minor ailments suggest irritations in your waking life; a serious illness may reflect a major hurt or concern.

In your dream: A minor problem, like a **bruise**, **ache**, **sting** or **rash** may mean someone has 'bruised your feelings' or given you 'heartache' in your waking life. Is someone irritating, like a stinging insect? Or have you done something silly that left you 'red-faced' with embarrassment?

Was the illness a serious one? A **heart attack**, for example, suggests that you have had your heart 'broken' by someone you had every right to trust, and are suffering greatly. A **stroke** may indicate that you are paralyzed by fear or anxiety. **Cancer** suggests that something is 'eating you up inside', or that something or someone malignant has wormed their way into your mind or emotions.

Treatment in a dream can suggest that you know how to solve the problem. Being inoculated, for example, indicates steps to prevent the problem taking hold. A **blood transfusion** suggests 'new blood' coming into your life and revitalizing you. An **operation** suggests you know you should 'cut out' the situation or person from your life.

(See also The Human Body, page 112, for suggested meanings for parts of the body, and what conditions affecting them might indicate)

Accident

Accidents can be insignificant or major: dreaming of them generally means your subconscious is warning you to take extra care in your waking life.

In your dream: Does the type of accident reflect an occurrence in your waking life? A **car accident**, for example, can mean either an accident in your car or in your sex life – perhaps an unwanted pregnancy. **Burning** yourself suggests you may be 'playing with fire' in a personal relationship, and should stop before anyone is hurt. Accidentally **poisoning** yourself is possibly a warning to take more care over your diet or any medication you may be taking. If you **cut yourself**, are you perhaps causing problems for yourself with your 'cutting wit' or sharp tongue? Dreaming of **breaking a bone** may indicate a need to be less clumsy, but which bone is broken also has a bearing on the meaning. Breaking your leg suggests you need to sit and take it easy for a while; breaking an arm that perhaps a little physical exercise which doesn't involve the use of your hands is in order. Dreaming of being **concussed** may simply reflect a wish to 'switch off' and forget your problems for a while, without feeling guilty.

Punishment

Most of us learn quite early in life that actions have consequences, and if our actions are what our society or our parents, consider bad or wrong, we will be punished. The precept stays with us throughout our lives.

There are, of course, other reasons why one person punishes another: to gain power over the other, to instil fear, to make the other feel inferior. Punishment can take a variety of different forms, not all physical.

In your dream: What were you punishing yourself for? A real transgression or an imagined one? To assuage your guilt? Because you've broken a self-imposed rule – to not eat chocolate on a diet, for example – or because you have committed a real crime? Your subconscious is likely to keep nagging you until you have either forgiven yourself for your action – if you are the only person involved – or gained a measure of absolution by doing what you can to heal the harm caused to another.
(See also Prison, jail, page 315; Violence, page 166)

Crime

More a nightmare than a dream. If you are the victim of crime, the dream may simply be an awful memory or a fear. If you are committing a crime, this is most often a means of gaining a measure of satisfaction for an insult or infringement of your own person or feelings. It should never be taken as a suggestion or licence to perform the actual deed.

In your dream: Were you a victim? Take practical steps in your waking life to ensure your safety [consider installing extra locks and alarms; find out who to contact in an emergency]. With the added security, your subconscious should accept the fact and the dreams should lessen.

Were you the perpetrator? Was the crime against a person, someone you know? Why would you want to rob or harm them? If it was against property, do you know the owner? Try to find parallels in your waking life.

Money

Money has become an indispensable part of our lives, and a source of passion, worry and despair for a large number of people.

In your dream: Being short of money may reflect your waking life finances. If you're comfortable financially yet still dream of being destitute, your subconscious may be pointing out that money isn't everything: are you lacking in social skills or personal qualities?

A dream of **winning a big cash prize** is usually simply wish-fulfilment!

Gambling

From buying lottery or raffle tickets to risking your life savings at a casino, gambling is always accompanied by the excited anticipation of a big win and the potential danger of losing. If you habitually gamble, or if it's becoming a problem, dreaming of gambling and losing is most likely to be your subconscious warning you to seriously consider the consequences of your hobby.

In your dream: It's unwise to take a dream of winning as an omen or good fortune: it may simply be wishful thinking, or a reminder that you've been lucky in 'life's lottery'.

Legal matters

A dream of being involved in legal matters is often simply a reflection of matters that are of concern in your waking life. If questions of property, wills, money, goods and so on are bothering you, you are very likely to dream of them.

In your dream: Did it reveal any way to resolve the problems? A way to compromise, perhaps, or some third party you can approach for help? If you dream of **making a will** and haven't yet done so, you might be wise to consider it – not because of any anticipated death or disaster, but just to set your mind at ease for the future.

Politics

We elect politicians to positions of power, and expect them to do what is best for us and the country. Sometimes this happens, often it doesn't, but politicians are nevertheless in the unenviable position of being unable to please most of the people most of the time.

In your dream: If you mentally switch off whenever the subject of politics is broached in your waking life, but politics makes a prominent appearance in your dreams, your subconscious may well be telling you to take some interest or become involved.
(See also Politician, page 188)

Blackmail, bribery

A dream of being blackmailed may denote a guilty conscience or a worry about a situation. Most people have had experience of bribery, even if only as a child by the promise of a sweet if they behave themselves.

In your dream: Have you done anything that could make you a blackmail victim? If so, your subconscious might be warning you that someone else is aware of the fact and could make problems for you. If you are blackmailing someone else, why? For the sense of power it gives you? For revenge? Because you're in financial difficulties?

To dream of being bribed or bribing someone else suggests that your current work is less than inspiring and you could do with something to 'sweeten' it.

Secrets, betrayal

Everyone has secrets. Revealing a secret to a friend demonstrates great trust; having that trust betrayed by gossip or rumour-mongering is very unpleasant.

In your dream: Were you entrusted with a secret? Did you keep it, or did you tell others – and if so, why? To save someone else pain, or to stop a crime being committed? Did you feel guilty?

Did you dream of someone giving away your own secrets? How did you feel about the betrayal – horrified, disillusioned? Consider whether the dream was your subconscious warning you that whatever you're keeping a secret may have serious repercussions.

Falsehood and fakery

Your subconscious is probably warning you that something you've accepted at face value is false and may prove harmful to you personally, to your reputation, your work or someone you know. Alternatively, you may be the source of the falsity.

In your dream: What was false in the dream? Was someone lying to you or trying to pass off a fake as real? If the latter, what did the object represent – a person, or something you value or would like to own? Consider what your subconscious may be trying to tell you.

Were you yourself the fake? Do you pretend to be something other than your real self in waking life? Were you discovered in the dream? Consider the consequences if the deception continues. It may be safer to tell the truth.

Hiding

Hiding can be a means of escape or of not facing something or something unpleasant (perhaps even an aspect of yourself) or of ducking responsibilities.

In your dream: What were you hiding from? Is someone or something threatening you in waking life, or asking you to do something you find distasteful? Or do you simply not want to face your problems?

If you were looking for someone but not able to find them, consider why they would hide from you. Are you asking too much of them? Are they afraid of you and if so, why?

(See also Running to Escape, page 144)

Struggle

Struggle seems to be an integral part of the human condition: from birth to death most of us will have to fight for our rights or beliefs or simply to be able to live, at some point.

In your dream: What are you struggling against? Does it involve an ill-defined 'enemy' such as society itself or is the opponent familiar, within you? Do you struggle with elements of your own character – laziness, perhaps, or anger? Are you fighting against authority, your parents, your boss, someone who has a claim on your time or resources? Does the dream give any indication of a way to lessen the conflict?

Phobias

Most people have something they fear, and in dreams these fears may be magnified. A claustrophobe may have a nightmare about being buried alive in a coffin; an arachnophobe may be stalked by elephantine spiders. But dreams may also be about conquering these fears – keeping your cool and digging your way out or frightening spiders into a corner.

In your dream: Was the phobia something that colours your waking life? With a little effort, you can use such dreams as a form of sleeping aversion therapy: by dealing with the problem while you are asleep, dealing with it when you are awake becomes easier.

Security and insecurity

If our early lives are secure and loving, personal insecurity is usually less of a problem in adult life and less likely to feature in dreams. Nevertheless, a sense of insecurity can be engendered by something as simple as going on holiday to an unfamiliar place, and will be reflected in dreams.

In your dream: Were you unable to find something essential to your personal security, such as **keys** or **wallet** or even the person you most rely upon? A dream of **locks**, a **guard** of some kind or an **alarm** may be suggesting steps you can take to improve your own security and that of your friends and family.
(See also Lock, Key, pages 300–301)

Rejection

Rejection is most painful; it leaves us with low self-esteem, a loss of self-confidence, and a lot of asking what we did wrong. Nevertheless, both to reject and to be rejected is something that is almost bound to happen to us all at least once in our lives.

In your dream: What form did the rejection take? A lover dropping you? A letter of refusal? How did you react – gracefully, angrily, with resignation? Did you decide to move on or did you beg to be accepted or taken back? Has this been your reaction in waking life? Has it proved successful or should you try to deal with it in another way?

Alternatively, were you rejecting something or someone? Is your subconscious telling you they are holding you back from fulfilling your potential? Rejecting someone is almost as unpleasant as being rejected, but it may be necessary to your emotional and mental health.

Personal loss

To dream of losing something is often a warning to take care of it in waking life if you don't want the dream to come true, but a real sense of loss is deeply distressing, in dreams as in waking life. The death of a loved one, human or animal, may be reflected in dreams by association – dark, miserable weather, a cemetery or an empty feeding bowl, for example. A loss of a personal quality – self-respect, innocence or confidence, perhaps – may be represented by giving or throwing something personal away, something you have made with your own hands, letters you have written, or possibly your virginity.

In your dream: If you cannot relate your dream to personal loss, did it involve a destructive actions such as shredding, burying or cutting up, applied to relevant symbols such as photographs or letters. This may refer to other people. A dream of burning a photograph, for example, may suggest that your respect for the person in it has 'gone up in smoke' and can never be regained, perhaps due to some disastrous or stupid action on their part.
[See also next two entries]

Loneliness, abandonment

Loneliness is often associated with loss. Alternatively, a dream of being or feeling lonely may suggest you feel that no one understands you or accepts you for who you are.

In your waking life: Has someone recently left you, either by dying or moving away? Have you become too dependent on just one person? Does the dream reveal any way to make your life easier?
[See also Friends, page 138]

Death

A dream of death can assume the quality of a nightmare, especially if it's your own. Unless someone you know is dying or has recently died, a dream involving death usually symbolizes major change, a movement from one phase of your life to another – a metaphoric 'dying' in your old form and being reborn in a new one.

In your dream: Do you feel that something in your life 'will be the death of you'? If so, does the dream give any indications of what it is, so that you can change it?
(See also Birth, page 157)

NIGHTMARES

Violence

Violence can take a number of forms, from verbal through physical to sexual, but it's always unpleasant. If you are in danger of actual violence in your waking life, this is likely to be reflected in your dreams. If so, it's vital to take steps to forestall the action or to stop it happening again. Obtain outside help and advice where possible.

In your dream: Dreaming of being violent towards others is most often indicative of anger and frustration that you cannot express, either because in waking life you find confrontation difficult or because it's directed towards something or someone out of your reach. Expressing the feelings in your dreams might be the only option, unless you can safely take action to resolve the issue.

Threat

The most nebulous of nightmares, a dream permeated by a vague feeling of threat, where everything seems to loom and intimidate. It may be caused by an atmosphere of mistrust or undefined fear in your waking life at work or at home, or simply by a problem that will need to be resolved. If it's a recurring dream it may be wise to examine it more closely.

In your dream: Is there anything that might suggest the cause of the threat? A person, perhaps, or an animal or object representing an individual or a concern? How can you change or improve matters?

Evisceration

The thought of having one's internal organs torn out is horrific. In dreams, it suggests either a distinct lack of self-confidence and feelings of unworthiness, or the feeling of being 'eaten alive' by those around you.

In your waking life: Is too much being demanded of you? Do colleagues and family expect you to give of yourself, your time and energy without thanks or credit? This last may be particularly significant if the dream involves carrion eaters. (See also Hyena, page 83; Vulture, page 97; Internal Organs, page 123)

Amputation

The significance of amputation depends on which part of the body was being cut off. Amputation forced on you may indicate your awareness of someone trying to take away that function, or take control of that aspect of your life or character. Choosing to lose a specific part of your body may indicate a subconscious wish to abdicate control or responsibility over whatever it is that that body part represents.

In your dream: What part of you was being amputated? Losing a leg, for example, may suggest you'd rather be absolved of the need to move around; your tongue, that you're tired of being the spokesperson all the time; or alternatively, that you're aware of hurting others by what you say and feel you should be stopped. Alternatively it may be a warning that unless you start using that limb or faculty, you run the risk, metaphorically, of losing it!
(See also The Human Body, pages 112–125)

Castration

Most men would prefer to lose any other part of their body before their penis or testicles, which represent masculinity, potency and legacy in the form of children. Dreams of being castrated symbolize having power taken from you forcibly. (Though rarer, women can dream of being castrated too).

In your dream: Are you afraid of losing your ability to satisfy a lover, losing a position of authority or losing your future?

If you are performing the castration, is it an expression of rage against an individual or against humanity in general? (See also Groin, page 121)

Rape

The ultimate physical invasion can never be condoned or excused. This abuse of power can cause hidden scars that last forever. You don't need to have experienced the ordeal to feel the horror in dreams.

In your dream: Being raped may indicate a subconscious awareness that you are in a dangerous or risky situation in waking life. Consider making some major changes.

Dreams of raping may indicate a deep loathing of whoever you are violating, or you may subconsciously feel inferior.

Torture

Torture can be performed for a purpose, such as attempting to gain information, or it can be done for its own sake.

In your waking life: Is someone pressuring you into telling secrets? Are you being cruel to someone because you've taken a dislike to them or because they're too timid?

5 OCCUPATIONS

In dreams everyone can be whatever they want. Generally, the more enjoyable the dream job, the more likely it is to be wish-fulfilment or your mind trying to cheer you up - being a successful model when your real job is behind a call-centre desk, for example. However, if you dream of enjoying an occupation not too far outside your skills and aptitudes, it may be worthwhile checking out its possibilities. If you dream of trying a new game or sport, try tackling it in waking life - it may enrich your working and social life as well.

Builder

Building – a home, a relationship, a family, a career – is one of the most basic occupations, as well as being a major motivator in your life. The state of the building is a good indicator of the state of the project, whether it was just starting, work in progress or a finished structure.

In your dream: What were you building? Were you working alone or as a team? Was it for yourself or for someone else? Was the project going well or were there problems? If your work was complete, was it well-built with sound foundations, or shaky and unsafe, or already collapsing? Does the dream give you any clues as to how to improve the structure or a more efficient way of working?
(If your dream involved tools, see also Tools, page 324)

Plumber

A plumber's job is practical and necessary, but it can also be an unpleasant one, dealing with blocked drains and sewers.

In your dream: Water usually symbolizes our emotions: are yours blocked at the moment? Or are you 'plumbing the depths' of your feelings for someone or something?

Electrician

Electricity is a dangerous force to be treated with respect, yet almost everything we use in our day-to-day life requires its power. Needing to call on an electrician's services in a dream suggests that your energy may be flagging or you feel 'powerless' and in need of a boost.

In your dream: What was the electrician working on? If it was your lighting, do you feel 'in the dark' and stumbling at the moment? Installing electrical sockets may suggest you are in need of more 'outlets' in your life. But if you were the electrician, it suggests you feel you are in control of your own inner energy, and are capable of dealing with life's circumstances.

Carpenter

Working with wood requires patience and skill. A carpenter also has Christian symbolism, as Jesus and his father Joseph were carpenters.

In your dream: Being or employing a carpenter suggests a wish to return to a slower, quieter life where due merit is given to traditional skills and those who possess them.

Glassworker

Blowing and working with glass is a very specialized skill, requiring a high level of artistry.

In your dream: To dream of blowing glass suggests you are or believe yourself to be capable of creating beauty out of the most fragile of things – not necessarily glass. Human minds, especially those that have been hurt or damaged in some way, can also be considered fragile.

Repairman, mechanic

Dreaming of being or dealing with a repairman suggests an unconscious acknowledgement that there are things in yourself or your life that need 'fixing'.

In your dream: Dreaming of something faulty in your home may be associated with a worry in waking life – if it's your stove, for instance, are you eating properly or feeding the family healthily? If it's an electronic device, do you feel you need advice and assistance with modern technology – your computer, for example? Dreaming of a mechanic fixing your vehicle can indicate a fear of delays in travelling or, if the car is a sexual symbol, a problem with your sex drive. (See also Car, page 195)

Farmer

Farmers are providers of food, one of life's most basic necessities. They may also represent living in harmony with the land and the animal world.

In your dream: Do others rely on you to provide nourishment, physical, emotional or spiritual? Or do you wish that they would, since you have so much to offer? Is the dream a reaction to a daily job that keeps you isolated from the natural world? You may need to take some time to reconnect with your 'roots'.
(See also Farm, page 319)

Shepherd

Shepherding carries a number of associations. Shepherds lead their sheep and are responsible for their welfare. Do you look after a 'flock' in waking life; children perhaps, or are you a manager or boss? Shepherds are out in all weather, in touch with nature and the animals they care for. The shepherd is also a symbol of Jesus in his role of the good shepherd taking care of his 'flock' of believers.

In your dream: Perhaps the romantic notion of the shepherd, crook in hand and faithful sheepdog at his side, appeals to the part of you that wishes life were simpler, more natural. Or are you looking for a shepherd or guide, someone to rely on, on whom you can lay your responsibilities and burdens?
(See also Lamb, page 77)

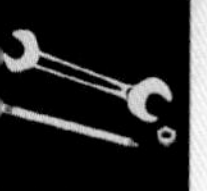

Fisherman, trawlerman

The sea in dreams generally represents the unconscious mind and our emotions. If you don't fish in waking life, a dream of fishing may indicate a desire to expose hidden emotions to the air in order to gain nourishment from them, examine them in the light and try to understand them.

In your dream: Are you perhaps being too clinical in waking life, analysing each feeling without relating it to the others?

Gardener

Gardening can be hard work, but is also very satisfying, working with nature in a small way to produce something beautiful and often useful.

In your dream: Are you trying to 'train' those around you, bring out their best aspects? Are they allowing it, or resisting? Are you 'weeding out' people or ideas that detract from your vision?
(See also Garden, page 318)

Woodsman, lumberjack

This is an occupation that takes you out into the wilds but gives you dominion over nature. Its associations in a dream can be similar to gardener, but on a larger scale.

In your dream: Dreaming of such an occupation suggests that you see yourself as responsible for 'cutting away the dead wood' in your job, perhaps planning on a large scale projects that won't come to fruition until after your time.
(See also Wood, page 20; Forest, page 20)

Sanitation engineer, garbage collector

Another of those necessary but unpleasant occupations. Dreaming of clearing away rubbish has obvious connections with doing the same in your waking life.

In your dream: Do you feel that your life is of no worth, that everything around you is rubbish? Or are you making a determined effort to clear away the trash in order to make a fresh start?

Teacher

A vital profession that shapes the next generation, teaching is still a vocation. Deciding to train as a teacher is a big undertaking. Dreaming of teaching even though it's not your job in waking life suggests you may have knowledge and skills you want to pass on to others.

In your dream: If the dream becomes so prominent that you believe it is urging you to become a teacher, make sure you have all the facts before embarking on any course. Consider also other ways you can realize the dream – tutor work colleagues on particular elements of your job, for example, or volunteer to train others in the evening.

Interpreter, translator, code-breaker, spy

These security-related occupations all involve revealing the unknown or discovering what is hidden, having a key to something – a foreign language, a mystery, a motivation – that others don't possess.

In your dream: A dream of being in one of these occupations may indicate an obsession with personal security, with making sure you are aware of the dangers posed by other people, and with understanding others' motives and motivations. Alternatively, it may suggest that you see yourself, or would like to be seen, as difficult to interpret, enigmatic, mysterious. A dream of being a spy suggests a lack of excitement in your waking life, a wish to experience a more daring, dangerous, seemingly glamorous way of life, even if only in your dreams.
(See also Code, page 234)

Reporter, newsreader

Reporters always strive to be first with the news or the gossip. They have a lively interest in what's happening in the world and in people's lives. Newsreaders, on the other hand, pass on rather than investigate, although they have a certain aura of glamour.

In your dream: A dream of being a reporter may suggest seeing yourself as a source of current events among those you know. It also indicates an energetic, enquiring mind. Dreaming of being a newsreader suggests you feel that you are restricted to repeating what other people have discovered, and may be frustrated or feel guilty with your role, despite its status.

Shop assistant

Not the most exciting of occupations, perhaps, but if your waking life job is high-powered and stressful, dreaming of being a shop assistant suggests that taking time out, or even looking for a less demanding, less pressured career, might be in order.

In your dream: In what sort of shop were you working? Anything to do with fashion or beauty may indicate that you might be feeling dowdy and in need of a makeover. A shop selling food, especially of the high calorie kind, may suggest an awareness that you need to lose some weight or start paying more attention to your diet.

Hairdresser, barber

Hair is often an individual's 'crowning glory' and allowing someone else to get their hands on it is an act of great trust. Do you occupy a position of trust for your friends, family and colleagues? Are you the person who always makes everyone else feel good about themselves?

In your dream: Were you making someone look smarter or more beautiful, or were you cutting manically? Such a dream may indicate you would like to exact revenge on someone by ruining their image, since hair takes an appreciable time to grow out and a bad cut can be a blight even for someone who isn't usually too concerned about their appearance. (See also Hair, page 117)

Salesperson

The role of a salesperson is to persuade others to buy, by making whatever is for sale seem attractive or essential. It can be a manipulative occupation.

In your dream: What were you trying to sell? Something useful or something useless? How does this reflect what you do in waking life? If you aren't a salesperson, it might be that your subconscious views your occupation as involving trying to 'sweet-talk' people into doing something they might find objectionable. If this troubles you, and if the dream is frequent, it might be worth your while investigating a different line of work.

Cook, chef

The best cooks take raw materials and almost magically turn them into wholesome, delicious meals, sometimes plain, sometimes sumptuous, but always nourishing.

In your dream: Dreaming of being a cook may indicate a wish to combine the raw materials of your life into something substantial. Consider how you can use your talents to your advantage. Alternatively, are you substituting food for love in waking life, eating for comfort? Should you offer larger servings of love to those close to you?
(Did a particular food feature large in the dream? If so, see also Food and Drink, page 261)

Manager

If you aren't a manager in waking life, do you feel that you could do better than your boss? Your subconscious may be reacting to the frustration caused by your manager in your daily occupation.

In your dream: Dreaming of being a manager is often more a stress-relief dream than a suggestion that you try to oust your waking life manager – although if you think you could do the job, you could always consider applying for the position!

Executive, chairman, director

A high-status executive post carries prestige, power and often wealth, but may be stressful.

In your dream: A dream of being a high-ranking executive in a company is more likely to be wishful thinking than anything else.

Image consultant, life coach

Dreaming of changing your image or your lifestyle, or actively changing someone else's, can suggest a powerful subconscious urge – the meaning of the dream will depend on whether you were the consultant/coach or the client.

In your dream: Do you wish to be able to take over and 'sort out' the lives of others? It's easy to see where other people are going wrong, but be wary of offering assistance where it may not be welcome!

Counsellor, psychiatric worker, psychiatrist

Do you have an urge to analyse other people, a desire to find out 'what makes them tick' in order to help them make the best of their lives? Dreaming of being on the receiving end of analysis or counselling may be a way of airing your innermost feelings to yourself, in order to straighten out your thoughts.

In your dream: Were you successful in helping someone else? Or was your dream a form of **confession**?

Decorator

Decorators may or may not be creative but they work with colour and make a room new, fresh and different.

In your dream: Are you trying to 'cover up' or 'whitewash' something in your life? Perhaps something you or someone of your acquaintance has done wrong? Or do you just yearn to add some colour to your life?
(See also Colours, page 255; Paint, page 332)

Nurse

Tending people when they are ill and nursing them back to health is associated with a caring nature, a desire to make others feel better.

In your dream: Were you looking after someone on their sick bed? If so, it suggests a capacity for empathy and a longing to bring comfort and ease to people. However, if the main accent was a too-tight, too-short uniform, then the dream is more likely to be related to sexual role-play.
(See also Hospital, page 314; Clothes page 283)

Doctor

Doctors are trusted to look after our health, make correct diagnoses and perform procedures designed to heal us. It's a huge responsibility. Doctors are seen as authority figures, skilled and knowledgeable beyond anything the normal, untrained individual can fully understand.

In your dream: Perhaps your subconscious is expressing a wish to heal someone close to you? Or is it more a wish to have life-or-death control, metaphorically speaking, over someone in your life?

Mortician, undertaker, gravedigger

Death and the dead are often a metaphor in dreams for a moribund cause or relationship, not necessarily a person. How do you feel about death and the dead in waking life? Does the thought of handling dead bodies repulse you?

In your dream: Were you involved in handling a dead body? Your subconscious may be telling you to let go of something – an affair, a project, an idea – that is dead but which you are still hoping may be reanimated. If you were digging the grave, you are probably ready to let go and are simply reassuring yourself that it's the right thing to do. (See also Death, page 165)

Childcare

Taking care of children, whether as a parent or someone else entrusted with their welfare, is an absolutely essential job if the next generation is to grow up happy, healthy, stable and well-adjusted.

In your dream: Dreaming of such an occupation reveals either a profound concern for children's future, or a wish to control them. If the latter is the case, it might be wise to seriously reconsider your relationship with the children. (See also Child, page 137)

Barkeeper, publican

The popular image of a person behind the bar is of someone who dispenses cheer, friendly interest and occasionally earthy advice, along with alcohol and snacks.

In your dream: Are you naturally a cheerful, popular person? If not, your dream may be indicating you would like to be.

Model

The image of the model, both male and female, is everywhere, trying to sell everything from clothes to cars. The life is glamorous but hard and short-lived.

In your dream: Dreaming of being a model generally indicates a wish for adulation, attention and the wealth that goes with a successful modelling career.

Jeweller

Jewellers work with expensive gem stones and precious metals to create beautiful, cherished articles to enhance the people who wear them. Jewellery is often a status symbol.

In your dream: What type of jewellery were you making? What materials were you using? Gems symbolize hopes, while metals symbolize relationships. Were you making the jewellery for yourself or someone else? Was the design modern and forward-looking, or traditional with strong links to your past? If you were paid for your work, does that reflect how well-rewarded you feel in your waking occupation? (See also Gems and Metals, page 64; The Human Body, page 112)

Animal carer

A dream of working with animals, as a breeder, animal nurse, trainer or zoo assistant, for example, can suggest a wish to get in touch with the animal side of yourself – in safe surroundings, as opposed to in the wild – or to protect the animals who are exploited by humans.

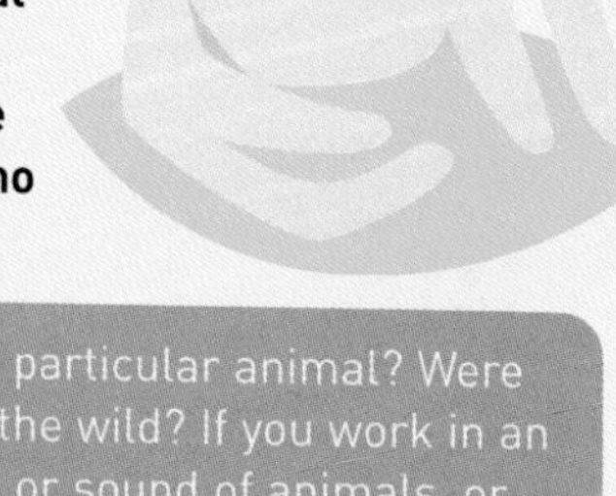

In your dream: Were you tending a particular animal? Were you in a domestic setting or out in the wild? If you work in an occupation removed from the sight or sound of animals, or have no pets, such a dream can be wish fulfilment. (See also Jungle, page 22; Creatures, pages 74–110)

Vet

The responsibility of treating hurt or ill animals requires different skills from that of a doctor, although the care needed during treatment is similar. If you have pets or animals of your own, dreaming of being a vet could indicate that you're worried about their health.

In your dream: Were you dreaming of your own animals? Maybe your subconscious has picked up clues that you aren't aware of physically. It might be wise to keep an eye on the animals involved and seek help if you think it's called for. (See also Doctor, page 182, substituting animals for people)

Bank staff

A dream of working in a bank may simply indicate that you have money concerns or financial problems. Alternatively it may suggest you have a keen business sense or that you see yourself as a doler out of money to others – this last is more likely if you have children!

In your dream: How did your dream role relate to your waking life? Was the emphasis on the job, or was it on the handling of money? Did you feel in control or overwhelmed? (See also Money, page 157)

Accountant, bookkeeper

Do you 'balance the books' in your waking life? Keep those around you on the 'straight and level'?

In your dream: Were you performing well or were there inaccuracies and inconsistencies? If so, can you pinpoint which aspects of your life need attention?

Lawyer

The legal profession is generally though not always respected and reputed to be wealthy, at least at the highest levels. A dream of being a solicitor or barrister may indicate a wish to adjudicate a particular problem in your waking life, one where an objective viewpoint is needed. Or it may be a form of wishful thinking or wish fulfilment, especially if your dream actions and judgements solved the case.

In your dream: Were you feeling helpless in a particular legal matter and asking for help? Or were you **sitting in judgement**? Perhaps you feel that your sense of justice isn't being given its due respect at work.
(See also Legal Matters, page 158)

Police force

Working for the police can be a thankless task, but it's also a vital one. Depending on your experience in waking life, the police may stand for law and order, safety or overbearing officiousness.

In your dream: Were you expressing your dissatisfaction with the way a personal problem has been handled? Or do you think you could 'do a better job' than the local force?

Politician, diplomat

Politicians and diplomats have rather different images, but both are concerned with acting as liaison between groups, and representing the rights of people.

In your dream: Did you feel you were acting as a representative for people and doing it well? Or that you were under a lot of pressure to act as intermediary between groups of people in your life – work colleagues, family, quarrelsome friends? The former may signify that you might be good in a job of this nature, but if the latter, can you delegate some of the responsibility?

Clockmaker

Clocks and watches are precision instruments and dreaming of making them suggests a keen appreciation of both time passing and the complexity of the mechanism.

In your dream: Do your days 'run like clockwork', smoothly and effortlessly, or is your life more like a broken clock, 'right twice a day' but otherwise frustratingly out of order? Do you wish you had more time in your day?
(See also Time, page 246)

Blacksmith

An ancient occupation, blacksmiths were the original weapon makers. To dream of working in such a fiery environment, hammering red hot metal into shape, suggests either confidence in your own strength, whether physical or mental, and ability to 'forge your way' in life.

In your dream: Forging and shaping metal suggests a wish to have control over whatever metal means to you – perhaps the 'iron hand' of a boss or superior, or a 'man of steel'.

Homemaker

Homemaking involves elements of a large number of other jobs including childcare, bookkeeping and nursing as well as being designer, cook, counsellor and diplomat. Multi-tasking skills are much in evidence.

In your dream: Were you floundering, unable to keep up with everything that needed doing? Are you in the same position in your waking occupation? Do your colleagues expect too much of you – a common reaction to anyone who shows themselves to be very competent. Or is the dream an expression of a wish to be able to work at home for a while, to face the challenges of self-discipline but free from the necessity to adhere to a dress code, drive into work, put up with workplace distractions and so on?

Auxiliary

The term covers all those little-regarded jobs that deal with the vital but unglamorous details of working life, and includes porter, clerical assistant, filing staff, shelf stocker, cleaner, technician, housekeeper, janitor, secretary and personal assistant.

In your dream: If your occupation in waking life is managerial or professional, it suggests that you may subconsciously feel you're not worth your salary!

Hunter

Hunting can be a means of survival or it can be something done as sport or pleasure. The former is likely to reflect concerns about basic needs in your waking life, while the latter is more likely to have a metaphorical sense of hunter and hunted in the world of business or love.

In your dream: Were you hunting for food? If you are experiencing financial problems at the moment your subconscious may be trying to reassure you that you will be able to provide for yourself and your dependants. Alternatively, if you were unable to catch anything, it might be wise to reassess your options.

If you were hunting big-game animals, were you acting illegally or culling overpopulations of animals? Is someone 'poaching' from you, perhaps trying to lure your partner away, or are you trying to steal someone from another? (See also Running to Escape, page 144; Plain, page 22)

Guide

Confidence in your ability in the dream suggests you are confident as a guide in your waking life; the reverse may suggests you are feeling lost or off-course. Are you responsible for guiding others in waking life as a tour guide, teacher or religious practitioner of some kind?

In your dream: What sort of guide were you – in a relatively safe environment like a museum or stately home or more perilous territory such as caves or mountains? Were you guiding others safely or had you gone astray? If the latter, perhaps you are harbouring doubts about your ability to do your job properly.

Prostitute

The significance of dreaming of being a prostitute depends in part on how you feel about the occupation in waking life.

In your dream: Were you horrified at finding yourself selling your body? Do you feel that you are having to 'sell yourself' in your waking life? Are you 'prostituting' yourself in your job? Are you afraid you might have to in order to live?

Alternatively, if you liked the dream, no matter how guiltily, do you have a relaxed attitude towards sex in your waking life? In effect, were you being paid for doing something you enjoy?

6 TRANSPORT AND TRAVEL

Whether from necessity or for pleasure, travelling is such a normal part of life that its appearance in dreams is common, especially if it takes up a lot of your waking life. Consider the feeling associated with the dream: excitement, enjoyment of the journey through life, trying to escape from something or perhaps boredom, as though you are just 'going through the motions'. How does this apply to your everyday life?

Walking

Walking is such a basic activity we tend not to think very much about it until we can't manage it any more! Whether in your dream you were walking towards or away from something is significant, as is the fact that you were walking and not running – it suggests a lack of urgency, no sense of danger, with regard to your goal.

In your dream: Were you purposefully walking towards or away from something in the dream? How did you feel?

Alternatively, were you walking but getting nowhere, as though you were on a treadmill? This suggests an awareness that you aren't achieving your aims. Consider what you can do to improve matters and make beneficial changes in your life.

Running

Running takes four basic forms: away from something, towards something, for pleasure or in competition. The meanings of running dreams are fairly straightforward, although it's important to note the circumstances and other elements of the dream.

In your dream: Were you pursuing a goal – promotion or another person? Running away from danger or a hostile situation? Trying to keep up? If you weren't succeeding, consider alternative courses of action you might take.

Running for the simple pleasure of feeling your body is under your control indicates a healthy attitude and a feeling of happiness with your situation.

Running and getting nowhere suggests you feel yourself on the 'treadmill' or like a rodent on an exercise wheel: reconsider what you want from life

(See also Running to Escape, page 144)

Motorbike

There's a great deal of romance associated with the motorbike: the freedom of the open road, the image of the easy rider, the speed, the hint of danger, the versatility of the machine – and the fact that it's less environmentally damaging than other forms of mechanized transport is an element in its favour as well.

In your dream: Dreaming of riding a motorbike may indicate a wish to get away from the mundanities of life and take off for a while, leaving your responsibilities behind.

Bicycle

Riding a bike in a dream can indicate a range of meanings, from happy memories of cycling holidays through subconscious suggestions of improving your fitness to fears of not being able to keep up with the hectic pace of life.

In your dream: When deciding what the dream means for you, consider the weather, the scenery, the amount of effort expended and whether you were enjoying yourself . A bicycle is usually a child's first mode of independent transport, so it can represent freedom and a way to escape from parental dependence to some degree. For adults it can represent freedom from a reliance on mechanized transport, and an environmentally and personally healthy way of getting about.

Car

A car can be more than a means of getting from A to B; it can be a symbol of how you'd like others to view you – cars can say 'rich', 'powerful' and/or 'sexy'. For many men, it's seen as an extension of their masculinity – or compensation for their lack of it. Before considering what a dream of travelling by car might suggest, decide what cars mean to you.

In your dream: A woman dreaming of driving a fast, powerful sports car may be subconsciously either trying to compete with the men in her life or imagining what it would be like to be masculine. A similar dream for a man may be wishful thinking, a way to boast about his potency or wealth, an image of competitiveness or compensation for feelings of insecurity or inadequacy.

Driving

Driving is becoming more and more skilled and dangerous as the amount of traffic on the road increases. The flip side of the coin is the sense of freedom, of being in control behind the wheel and enjoying the frequent changes of scenery.

In your dream: Were you on a journey for pleasure with a **clear road ahead**? Or was your dream journey fraught with frustrations, even **gridlocked**? Is life proceeding smoothly, or are you facing obstacles at every turn? What can you do to improve matters? If a bicycle was moving faster than you, zipping through the traffic with ease, your subconscious might be suggesting that you need to be more self-reliant. (See also Accident, page 155)

Dreaming of being a chauffeur or taxi-driver suggests that you feel competent to cope with life's journey. Alternatively, are you trying to escape from a person or a situation?

Motorway and freeway

Motorways can be a very fast and direct way to get from one place to another, but they are hardly the most interesting of roads, especially if you're driving and need to keep your wits about you. Dreaming of driving along a motorway suggests either that you're set on your path and determined to get to your final goal or that you're stuck on your path and unable to get off.

In your dream: Were you **racing** in the dream, either with another car or to escape from pursuit, consider if you are a competitive person or if you'd rather let others compete, while you settle for a less dramatic, but also less stressful, life path. If you were **fleeing from the police**, ask yourself what you have to feel guilty about!

Train

Trains allow for a certain freedom of movement and from responsibility, but are literally 'one-track' vehicles, aiming for a definite and predetermined destination.

In your dream: Dreams of trains, especially of being on the **wrong train** or of a **journey delayed**, suggest a subconscious awareness that you might be limiting yourself by not exploring other, more attractive or beneficial goals and possibilities.

Dreaming of being in a **train crash**, especially if the dream recurs, may indicate that you know, subconsciously, that the path you're on is leading to disaster. In such an instance, it might be wise to consider other options.

Train station

Generally speaking, train journeys are a lot more limiting than sea or air expeditions, so dreaming of being in a train station suggests that while you are about to move ahead with something new, it's in a modest way – a decision to make some small changes in your life, perhaps.

In your dream: If the **train leaves without you** or if it thunders through the station **without stopping**, are you afraid that you've 'missed the train' in some way? Not been able to take advantages of the opportunities you wanted? Is there any way you can correct the situation?

Bus

Buses are prosaic forms of transport, but cheap, effective and environmentally friendlier than many cars.

In your dream: Waiting at a bus stop may indicate an inner awareness of having 'missed the bus'.

Ship

A slow method of transport, though enjoyable if the vessel is a **cruise ship** and you aren't in a hurry. The sea typically symbolizes the depths of the unconscious mind, and sailing on it suggests a tentative willingness to 'test the waters' without getting your feet wet.

In your dream: Travelling by ship may indicate a yearning for a slower pace of life or alternatively, it may reflect frustration in your waking life that you aren't achieving your aims as quickly as desired.
(See also Sea, page 29)

Sailor

What is your vision of a sailor in waking life? Do you conjure up an image of a naval rating or officer, or a merchant seaman? A trawlerman or a pirate? A submariner or the crew on a pleasure voyage? What, instinctively, do you associate a sailor with: fighting in battle? Trading? Helping people enjoy their voyage? Fishing? Involved in research or subterfuge below the waves or banditry above it?

In your dream: Think about how your dream scenario related to your most immediate image of a sailor. How does that relate to how you view yourself? Are you using your innate abilities to help others or harm them?

Harbour, port

Harbours and ports mark the transition point between living or working on land and living or working at sea. They are busy, bustling places, filled with a sense of purpose and sometimes urgency, and they have associations with starting out on a journey and the promise of new horizons.

In your dream: A vivid dream of **boarding a ship** at a harbour may suggest a yearning to make a major change in your working life, possibly even to move to another country to make a new start. If you're unhappy with your current partner, it may also suggest a desire to leave a stagnant relationship by 'sailing off', rather than trying to repair it. (See also Airport, page 201)

Anchor

An anchor prevents a vessel from drifting into danger, but it also halts any forward movement. In a dream, being anchored can mean either that you feel safe and secure in your life or that weighty matters are holding you back.

In your dream: An anchor in isolation may suggest that you feel adrift, with no way to control your life. Alternatively, especially if you've grown up in the tradition, it may also suggest hope: the anchor represents hope in the Christian imagery of faith, hope and charity.

Travelling by plane

Flight has always been one of the greatest dreams of the human race, to move through the air like the birds. The speed and ease with which we can now move over the face of the planet has changed our perception of the world forever. Air represents your aspirations and wishes, so flying symbolizes your attempts to fulfil them.

In your dream: Dreams of travelling by plane usually indicate ambition and the desire to rise above the problems in your life, leaving them behind on the ground. Such dreams may also suggest your ability to rise in your chosen profession – even if the thought of flying so high is a frightening thing! (See also Flying, page 143)

Pilot

When you are doing the flying rather than being a passenger, the type of plane can be significant: a large commercial airliner whose passengers trust you with their lives; a fighter jet defending your own country or attacking another; or a small plane carrying cargo, spotting fires or taking tourists up for a flight. The dream may reflect a responsibility you feel for ensuring other people's dreams are fulfilled at work or at home, or you are busy defending your own ideas in the workplace?

In your dream: Was the flight smooth and relatively trouble-free, or was it beset by problems? The latter suggests you are having difficulties achieving your objectives. Perhaps shedding a few people or some of the load you're carrying – responsibilities you've taken on that could be handed over to others – would make it easier to reach those goals.

Aircrew

Dreaming of being part of an aircraft's crew indicates that you feel you're supporting someone else's progress towards their goals. This is fine if the matter at hand is a company project, but perhaps less beneficial if you have your own goals that are being subsumed by your work.

In your dream: Were you happy with the situation? If not, is there anything you can do to change it?

Airport

Dreams of waiting for or boarding planes at an airport can have a similar meaning to harbours, except that they apply more to your professional or spiritual aspirations than your physical or emotional ambitions – your 'taking off into the wide blue yonder'. Such a dream isn't uncommon at the start of a new project or phase of your life.

In your dream: If the plane was delayed, consider if you've been putting off making decisions in this field. Are you perhaps delaying starting a course that would prove of use because of some underlying fear that you aren't capable – or worthy – of success?

Spacecraft

Perhaps the ultimate in man-made structures, a dream of being in a space vehicle of some kind, either in a spacecraft or on a space station, indicates a deep trust in the skills of those who shape the technology of the modern world, as well as the willingness to travel great distances in the search for personal fulfilment.

In your dream: Dreams of leaving the planet, going into orbit or travelling through space or to other worlds suggest the ability and willingness to leave behind everything familiar in order to be part of a awe-inspiring adventure into the future, whether in your waking life or within your own mind. Thrilling or frightening, such a dream often leaves a long-lasting memory.

An alternative meaning may be that you feel detached or isolated from waking reality, caught in 'a world of your own', maybe as a reaction to unpleasant personal circumstances.

Astronaut

Probably the most rarefied of occupations, the sheer glamour connected with the image of an astronaut has made it a not uncommon dream.

In your dream: Usually this suggests a deep wish to escape the ordinary, to be far above and beyond the normal, working about as high above the planet as is possible. The hard work and danger that goes with the job tends to be forgotten!

Hot-air balloon

An elegant, graceful and quiet way to fly, balloons can also be hazardous: while the gas used in modern times isn't as explosive as that originally employed, the risk of landing in an unfavourable place is real.

In your dream: What impressed you most? The sensation of floating or soaring? The link to the earliest flyers? Perhaps you want to rise in your career, but quietly and elegantly?

7 ENTERTAINMENT AND SPORT

What we do with our leisure time says a lot about the sort of person we are – energetic participant or passive observer, focused and enthusiastic or idly watching. If your dream reflects the opposite of your usual pursuits, is your subconscious suggesting you need to try something different? An intellectual hobby rather than an active one or vice versa?

Actor

Actors are associated with fame and being 'a well-known face', but acting also involves taking on another persona, hiding behind a disguise, sometimes literally. Many actors say they feel free to express themselves in character in a way they find difficult as themselves.

In your waking life: Are you acting a role, putting on a mask, hiding your true self? Why? For protection? Because you don't want anyone to get to know the real you? If so, why not? Do you find it exciting playing different roles? Are you exploring different elements of your personality? Or do you wish for the glamour, wealth and celebrity-status of being famous?

(See also Theatre, page 207; Cinema, page 208; Celebrity, page 207; Performing but Unprepared, page 146)

Illusionist, magician

Illusionists deal with unreality. Are you having trouble facing up to your responsibilities in waking life, preferring to pretend everything is fine? It might be better to pierce the veil of illusion before someone else does it for you, as they are unlikely to do so kindly.

In your dream: Dreaming of entrancing audiences with your 'magical' abilities may make for excellent entertainment, but if those skills were used to deceive others, are you doing something similar in your waking life? Do you have a secret wish to 'fool all of the people all of the time'?

Dancer

The rhythmic movement of the body to music is a very ancient art form, and dance ranges from the traditional formality of ballroom and classical ballet, through tap, jazz, and ice-dance, to pole-dancing. Dancing can be sensuous, fun, energetic or disciplined, but it's always an expression of your inner self.

In your dream: What sort of dance was involved? Is it something you practise in waking life or a style of movement you've never tried before? If you enjoyed it, perhaps you might consider taking classes! Were you dancing for pleasure, for money, for a demonstration? Were you teaching someone else? Did you have an audience or were you dancing purely for your own pleasure or even dancing on the inside where no one can see? What does this tell you about yourself? Are you happy to express yourself in public, as long as it's within recognized limits? Or would you prefer to give your body free reign to communicate your emotions? Or was the dance something you didn't like? Your mind may be telling you to consider a change of activity: you may need to dance to a different tune.

Celebrity

Celebrity here means someone who, by dint of appearing to large numbers of the general public, is well-known and recognized: the term includes the apparently ordinary people who appear on reality TV or in commercials.

In your dream: A dream of being 'famous' with no real ability to back it up indicates little more than a wish to be recognized, to receive some attention, and suggests that you are taken for granted in waking life.

Theatre

Whatever may be performed on the stage, theatres all have two things in common: they provide entertainment, and they present people 'acting out' roles that may be completely different from their real selves.

In your dream: Were you performing, managing from 'behind the scenes', or watching? Do you prefer to be 'up on life's stage', 'in the limelight', keeping things running smoothly, or do you simply like watching what others do?
(See also Actor, page 205; Performing but Unprepared, page 146)

Funfair

We visit funfairs for a thrill, or to be scared in a usually safe environment.

In your dream: Did you find the fair exciting or frightening – are you a risk-taker or do you prefer the safer course? Did you feel 'lost in the crowd', or happy to be surrounded by like-minded people?

Cinema

Films take you out of yourself, allowing you to enter another world and experience, albeit at second-hand, things impossible to you in your day-to-day life. By extension the cinema has become an almost magical place, where dreams and nightmares can come true on the screen. At the same time the cinema is a social place: seeing a film with a partner or a group of friends can be a special occasion.

In your dream: Being at a cinema, especially by yourself, suggests a wish that you could escape into the world portrayed on the screen, at least for a little while. What sort of film were you watching? If it was not one you would normally enjoy, does this imply that there's an area of your life that could do with some attention – your love life, for example, if you normally prefer action films and found yourself watching a romance? If you were there with a partner and paying at least as much attention to each other as to the film, perhaps the relationship could benefit from a little excitement.

Circus

The circus is life writ large. It is full of clowns and showmen, all bright lights, spangles and insubstantiality, but also the result of hard work, skill and dedication. Each act has its own character.

In your dream: Was there a particular act that caught your attention? The **high-wire artists**, perhaps – do you aspire to be a 'high-flyer' yourself? Or the **bareback rider**, whose superb physical control and sense of balance acieves intricate feats of strength and expertise at speed? Perhaps you identified with the **clowns**, 'clowning around', bringing laughter into people's lives. Are you a **fire-eater**, **sword swallower** or **juggler** with chainsaws, executing awe-inspiring stunts with daring skill? Or would you rather be the **ringmaster** in control of the whole event?

Chess

Chess is an ancient game of strategy. It can be seen as a battle between two opposing armies, a quiet but intense combat, requiring concentration, skill and finesse, and the wilier and more experienced of the two will be the winner. It's also a game in which the Queen is the most powerful piece on the board, far more so than the King. Playing chess in a dream suggests you are involved in some kind of struggle for dominance, most likely with one other person – your lover or boss, perhaps.

In your dream: What was the state of play on the board? This gives an indication of how well or badly you are doing. If you were losing, you're probably losing the battle in waking life as well.

Playing cards

There is a wide variety of both games and interpretations.

In your dream: Is your subconscious suggesting you'd be wise to put on a 'poker face' when dealing with other people, especially where your work or money is concerned? If you were playing bridge, should you perhaps have been 'building bridges' with the other people at the table? Are you happy playing solitaire or would you prefer to be part of a team? Were you dealt the joker – perhaps you suffer from malicious jokes in your waking life? Or are you the King or Queen of your social circle?

If you were losing money, you might be wise to reconsider any gambles you plan to take in waking life.

(See also Gambling, page 158)

SPORTS AND OUTDOOR ACTIVITIES

Sports in general

Most sports contain an element of hopefully friendly competition. Dreaming of being a sportsman or woman is likely to reflect a desire to win in your waking life, or the wish to be part of a team, or possibly – since sports personalities, like models and actors, are in the public eye more than the average person – a wish for adulation.

In your dream: Were you competing and did you win? Who were you playing against? Are you so competitive in waking life that it carries over into your dreams? Or are you rehearsing a game or sporting event in your mind? If you're usually sedentary, is your subconscious advising you to become more active and develop more of a social life? If you're playing a team sport, should you become more of a 'team-player' in waking life? Or perhaps strike out on your own if your team keeps losing! A dream of indulging in **extreme sports** is most likely to be wish-fulfilment, a vicarious enjoyment of the adrenaline rush that accompanies danger.

Martial artist

The oriental martial arts are notable for their speed, deadliness and extraordinary, almost supernatural abilities. To dream of using the skills, if you aren't a practitioner in waking life, suggests a wish to be able to tackle 'whatever life throws at you' with skill and aplomb.

In your dream: Were you a teacher or combatant? The former may indicate confidence in your abilities to deal with life leading to a preference for taking a less aggressive role; the latter can suggest the determination to stand up for your ideals and beliefs.

Swimming pool

If the swimming pool and not just swimming is a notable feature in your dream, it may add to the meaning. A pool represents somewhere relatively safe to swim, with an edge to hold on to if you feel tired. Perhaps it is a place for you to draw attention to yourself and your body or your swimming or diving skills? Or is it a place to train?

In your dream: Are you in competition with others, in your waking life as in the dream? Is your subconscious advising you to relax, take some gentle exercise and get in touch with your emotional side?

If you dream of **diving**, are you perhaps 'diving into' projects or relationships in waking life, throwing yourself willingly into action with enthusiasm? Or were you pushed?

Swimming

Generally speaking, swimming dreams represent your life and personal circumstances and how you're dealing with them. However, it also partially depends on whether you are able to swim in real life, and the circumstances in which you are swimming.

In your dream: Were you in a swimming pool, or were you at nature's mercy in the sea or a river? Was the water comfortable or were you fighting waves and currents? If you can swim in waking life but couldn't in the dream, are you struggling to cope with life, floundering, 'out of your depth' or feeling yourself 'cast adrift'? Conversely, if you're a non-swimmer but swimming confidently in the dream, it suggests that you are in control of your life, even if the 'water' around you is rough and unsafe.

If you're **swimming under water**, are you trying to delve into your own feelings and psyche? If you are **in difficulties** – unable to reach the surface, almost out of air – do you feel that you are 'drowning' in waking life, being swamped by responsibilities and obstacles? What can you do to alleviate the problem?

(See also Swimming pool, page 212; Sea, page 29 and other watery places in The Natural World, pages 19–73)

Surfing

Dream-surfing may be simply a happy memory or wishful thinking, or your mind may be trying a virtual 'dress rehearsal' to check you won't be wasting time or money. However, if the dream has come out of nowhere, it may indicate that you are happily skimming along the surface of life without much care or interest in the deeper aspects.

In your dream: Did you fall off the surfboard or start **sinking**? Your subconscious might be suggesting you start taking things a little more seriously.

Scuba-diving, snorkelling

Anything that will help you to breathe under water while still being in intimate contact with the element symbolizes a certain control over your emotional response to situations in your waking life.

In your dream: Whether you're consciously aware of it or not, you're easy with your feelings, and quite likely able to express yourself calmly, without sounding overwrought.

Ice -skating

Gliding across the ice can be an exhilarating release from the everyday plod of walking, and ice hockey and speed skating are fast and furious. But being on skates can also make you feel out of control, as your feet slide out from beneath you. And being out on pond or lake ice can be risky, especially if the ice is thin.

In your dream: Were you in control, gliding along gracefully or continually falling over? Are you in control of your waking life or flailing about, unable to keep your balance? If you were skating on thin ice, are you taking risks in your waking life? Or is the dream telling you to 'get your skates on' before you miss out on an opportunity to improve your life?

Climbing

Climbing has many grades of difficulty and this will reflect the level of effort and struggle in your dream. There is an obvious and important distinction between climbing towards something and climbing to escape.

In your dream: Were you striving to reach something, some goal that will take real effort to achieve? Or were you trying to get away from something? Frequent dreams of climbing may indicate a very ambitious nature – especially if the dream involves climbing over other people.

Horseriding

A dream of riding a horse or other animal relates to control of the animal, instinctive side of yourself.

In your dream: Were you in control of the horse or were you just clinging on during a runaway gallop? Were you fully equipped with hard hat, saddle and tack or **riding bareback**? The latter implies that while you can direct your less sophisticated urges, you aren't fully in control of them. (See also Horse, page 76; Circus, page 209)

Camping

A dream of going camping suggests a wish to get closer to nature, but without giving up all the benefits of civilization. The equipment you have with you may indicate the degree to which you are prepared to 'rough it'.

In your dream: Did you have a **tent** for protection from the weather, **sleeping bags** and **camping stove** for warmth and food, **maps** and **compass** to prevent you getting lost? All imply careful forethought and preparation, and suggest that you don't take risks in your waking life.

Gymnasium, sports hall, bowling alley

Dreaming of taking part in a sporting activity within the confines of a building suggests a more restrained 'half-way house' approach to exercise and to life?

In your dream: If you tend to a more sedentary life, a dream set in a location like this suggests you should become more active, though because this is an indoor area it will be less of a shock for you than starting a strenuous outdoor activity.

Parachute

Dreaming of using a parachute suggests that you expect to 'fall' in your current job or project, but are prepared and have taken steps to make sure you have a way out. This further implies a good degree of self-confidence and self-reliance, whether you are consciously aware of it or not.

In your dream: Were you still in the plane or were you already adrift? Were you in freefall or was the parachute open? Were you enjoying the floating sensation or did you feel panicky? Your reactions are likely to reflect your concerns over a 'jump' or 'fall' in your waking life.
(See also Flying, page 143; Plane, page 200)

8 WARFARE AND WEAPONRY

Dreams of conflict and war can be complex, and the context should be borne in mind. If, for example, you dreamed of climbing a mountain while carrying a weapon, are you prepared to do anything at all to achieve your ambitions, even if it means threatening or hurting others? Was the weapon associated with close, face-to-face combat, or was it of the coldly impersonal, kill-at-a-distance variety?

Rebellion, revolution

Rebellion pushes boundaries, tests limits, kicks against authority. Revolution is the ultimate rebellion, the overthrow of the old order to usher in a new one.

In your dream: Were you rebelling against something or was someone rebelling against you? Why? Are you feeling frustrated with the restrictions in your life?

Dreaming of being involved in a revolution indicates a desire to make major changes in your life, even so far as to emigrate or possibly have a sex change.

Conflict – fight, battle, war

If you have not experienced such conflict in your waking life, a dream of being involved in a fight or war can indicate internal conflict (will you or won't you take that action), fear of aggression, a cut-throat attitude towards others who are vying with you for the same thing – job, award, person – or an overwhelming feeling of hopelessness with the state of the world. Your feelings in the dream are important for deciding what it means to you.
(See also Struggle, page 162)

In your dream: Are you fighting for something – your partner, family, job, for example – or against something, loss, depression, frustration, redundancy? Does the dream reveal a way of dealing with the actual situation that doesn't involve a fight or is conflict inevitable? If you dream you are a **soldier**, are you winning or is 'the enemy' overcoming your defences? Does the dream provide any clues as to how you can be victorious?
(See also Pilot, page 200)

Weapons (general)

Weapons can be used for threat, attack or defence. It's important to bear in mind that weapons symbolize violence in one form or another, and often sexual violence. Frequent or recurrent dreams featuring weapons and their use may indicate an underlying emotional or mental problem that should perhaps be given professional attention.

In your dream: The landscape in which the dream takes place is significant. If the threat or attack took place in familiar surroundings, is there someone in your social or working life who you find threatening or whom you can't abide? Were you being threatened or attacked or were you the one on the offensive? If the surroundings were unfamiliar, do you find change or the unknown threatening?

Any weapon making an appearance in a dream of home suggests a willingness to defend yourself or your home and family, with violence if necessary.

Knife

A knife used as a weapon is easy to hide, and hence difficult to predict or plan for.

In your dream: Who used the knife? If it was someone else, is your subconscious warning you to be wary of them? If it was yourself, are you 'backstabbing' someone, or do you feel the need to carry something to protect yourself?
(See also Household equipment – Knife, page 335)

Sword

Swords are ancient weapons, varying from the light and flexible epée used in fencing, to the massive two-handled sword employed to hack enemies to pieces in battle. Swords can have a certain romanticism – for instance, Arthur's famous Excalibur, the mythical sword pulled from the stone and returned to the Lady of the Lake upon Arthur's impending death. The sword is also a symbol for the penis.

In your dream: What was the sword being used for – attack, defence or threat? Or perhaps as a display item in a castle or in a knighting ceremony – both indicative of conferred honour or nobility. Was it being used against you or for your protection by another? If the latter, do you want a 'knight' to look after you? If you were using it yourself, who were you protecting?

If you view the penis as a weapon, the image of a sword, especially one wielded threateningly, may have this meaning in dreams, especially if you are afraid of sex or have found it painful in the past.

Bow and arrows

A highly efficient ancient form of weaponry that's also associated with love and desire in the form of Cupid and his arrows. The bow is generally perceived as a hunter's weapon and, like the sword, enjoys a certain mythical and romantic reputation, probably because of its association with Robin Hood, Amerindian braves and fantasy creatures such as elves.

In your dream: Were you hunting? If so, what was your quarry? A new partner or lover? If it was an animal, which one (see also Creatures, page 74) Or were you being hunted? By whom? Were you happy about the situation or trying to escape?
(See also Being Attacked, page 146)

Spear

Spears are generally used for stabbing at a distance, preventing the opponent from getting close enough to use a shorter weapon. It takes considerable skill to throw a spear and hit a target, especially a moving one.

In your dream: Are you trying to keep someone at a distance, defending your 'personal space'?
(See also Being Attacked, page 146)

Boomerang

The boomerang is the only thrown weapon that returns to the thrower. It represents the consequences of your actions.

In your dream: Throwing a boomerang is likely to act as a warning that you should think very carefully before taking any action that can't be undone.

Battering ram

A blunt instrument used primarily to break down doors.

In your dream: What or who is trying to force itself into your life without your agreement?

Gun

At close quarters it doesn't require much skill to use a gun: hit any part of the body and you'll cause considerable damage, if not death. The gun is a male sexual symbol because of its shape and action. If you're female and usually non-aggressive, carrying or using a gun in a dream can indicate a wish to be more assertive, to be more 'masculine'. A gun can also represent a sexual threat: just as bullets can be life-threatening, semen can have life-altering consequences (pregnancy, but also sexually transmitted diseases).

In your dream: Were you defending yourself and if so, against what? Is someone or something threatening you in your waking life, so much so that your subconscious is suggesting violent and definitive action is needed to resolve the situation? Or do you feel you're 'looking down the barrel of the gun' in your personal or work circumstances? Perhaps you're facing redundancy with no alternative work options available, or you've discovered you have some life-changing illness. Did the dream show you any way out?

Rifle

Effectively a larger gun, generally used by military personnel or game hunters. Rifles are a particularly threatening type of gun to dream about.

In your dream: If you are using a rifle or being menaced by one, the waking life situation that sparked the dream is probably more extreme.
(See also Being Attacked, page 146 for more suggestions)

Cannon

An old but effective weapon, mostly used for blowing holes in castle walls, ships and the like.

In your dream: A cannon generally indicates that you feel under attack by a man or men and not in a subtle way. Are you being subjected to crude jokes or harassment at work? Did the dream reveal any way you can counter the attacks?

Missile, torpedo

Both of these attack from a distance, usually from an unseen enemy.

In your dream: Is someone 'targeting' or 'torpedoing' your ideas? Are you doing the same to someone else?

Explosive weapons – grenades, mines, bombs

We use these in our waking life as metaphors for danger or devastation. A weapon of mass destruction such as an atomic bomb affects whole populations, if not the planet as a whole. A nightmare of those proportions generally reflects a deep fear and mistrust of the science that created the weapons and the politicians and military that control them.

In your dream: Are you 'walking through a 'minefield' at work or in your personal relationships? Has someone 'dropped a bombshell' in your waking life recently? Does the dream reveal any way you can resolve the situation?

Stealth weapons

These include chemical and biological weapons, poisons and booby traps.

In your dream: Dreaming of succumbing to an unseen danger suggests an underlying fear of concealed threat, possibly from the modern environment or from something you are doing to yourself. Check your diet for toxins or addictive additives. If you are the one using the weapons, are you trying to 'poison' the atmosphere at work or the life of another?

Futuristic weapons

Weapons development is an integral if unwelcome part of life. They may not yet exist, but if they can be imagined, someone will devise a way to build them. Potential large-scale weapons, often based in orbit, can be positive and beneficial – to deflect meteors or falling space debris, for example – but in the main they are perceived as being intended for destruction on a massive scale.

In your dream: The setting is important – was it familiar or alien? Was the weapon recognizable – a cutting and cauterising laser or light-sabre, for example, or something mysterious? Were you using it to protect yourself or others, or was it being used against you? Were you in control or powerless?

9 KNOWLEDGE

Knowledge comes in many shapes and forms, and encompasses every field of human life. It can be passed on orally, in word or song, in pictures, in books or as visual or aural media. It provides us with our history and our ongoing technology. Included here are the basics that shape our knowledge – numbers, colours, time – and also areas of knowledge such as science and history and the people who work in them.

SCIENCE AND TECHNOLOGY

Given the profound effect ever-developing science and technology have on everyone's life, dreaming of them isn't unusual. Consider the level of your own knowledge and attitude being reflected in your dreams.

Science

Does the idea of 'science' summon up life-saving medicines or the horror of modern weaponry? The ability to look deep into space or to create deadly viruses? Being comfortably involved in anything scientific suggests an awareness of the importance of technology in modern life. Alternatively, you may dream about it if you're afraid of the way it impacts on your life.

In your dream: Consider what sort of science was concerned and what you were actually doing, then check other entries for further information. Do you have a reason to be grateful to or mistrustful of technology? Or is someone trying to 'blind you with science' to disguise their true motivation?

Laboratory

Despite how threatening laboratories can appear to the uninformed, they have produced amazing medical treatments, more efficient forms of energy and a deeper understanding of the universe.

In your dream: Was the laboratory modern and sterile, filled with bubbling test tubes and smelling of chemicals or a cobwebby dungeon from an old horror film? What does this teach you?

Scientist

A dream of being a kind of scientist may indicate a fascination with the particular discipline or with the idea of science as a whole.

In your dream: A **chemist** suggests an underlying concern with drugs and their effects, and may indicate a wish for more control over any medicines you take.

Biologists deal with the body: do you have a particular worry about a part of your own body? Are you perhaps wishing that you could use the latest science to engineer a change in yourself or someone close to you?

Physicists are associated with the forces of nature and, by extension, how to harness them. If you understandably fear humanity misusing this ability, a dream of being involved in physics may be a way of feeling more in control, or as an expression of a desire to understand it.

(See also Astronomer, page 232)

Astronomer

Astronomers see into the deepest reaches of space and probe the limits of humankind's knowledge about the universe.

In your dream: Dreaming of being an astronomer usually indicates a wish to explore the furthest reaches of your universe, perhaps in the hope or fear of discovering alien life.
(See also Space, pages 36–41)

Computers and computing

It's difficult to avoid having some contact with computers these days, even if it's only at the supermarket till. Dreams involving computers tend to be either frightening, where the machine starts wars, traps people or creates a nightmarish vision of runaway technology, or soothing, where the computer makes life easier. The former is more likely if you've experienced the results of a computer glitch and been left feeling powerless.

In your dream: If you use a computer on a regular basis, using one in a dream is likely to be no more than a hangover from your waking life, unless something strange was happening on screen. Did you see **gremlins** on it? Or the '**ghost in the machine**'?

Or did you dream up a new and innovative design for something? Can you reproduce what you saw on paper? Can you use it in any way?

Did you press the wrong button and irretrievably do something terrible? Dreaming of being unable to use a computer suggests a fear of losing control of your life, being at the mercy of other people. Learning how a computer operates may assuage the fear to some degree.

Microscope

Microscopes magnify very small things to a size where they can be easily seen.

In your dream: Are you 'under the microscope' at work or in your personal life? Is someone scrutinizing you minutely, to the extent where you feel unable to hide or escape?

Alternatively, are you using a microscope to examine other people or even elements of yourself?

Telescope

Telescopes, whether optical or radio, earth-bound or in space, look into the distance and bring close the images of things far away.

In your dream: Using a telescope may suggest that you are searching for something which you believe may be at a great distance from you.

Code

In one form or another, codes influence every aspect of our life, from our genetic code to the bar-codes on our shopping and the binary code that operates the computers. But codes in dreams are more likely to take the form of personal communication.

In your dream: What sort of code was it? **Morse code** suggests someone is trying to communicate with you urgently – did you understand what they were trying to say? **Written code** indicates secrets, yours or another's. Are you involved with someone or something you don't want to be generally known?
(See also Codebreaker, page 177)

Puzzle

Puzzles range from games to unfathomable enigmas.

In your dream: Dreaming of attempting a puzzle suggests you're struggling to understand something puzzling in waking life. Did you solve the puzzle? If so, how? Does that give you any clues as to how to solve the larger puzzle?
(See also Maze, page 321)

Map, globe

Maps and globes represent the planet on which we live: they present an overview, an image of the whole picture. In dreams they may also symbolize the frailty of the world and how easy it could be to pollute or destroy it, making it uninhabitable.

In your dream: Were you using a map to plan a journey or locate a particular place? Maybe you are feeling restless and in need of new scenery. Are you searching for a new place to call home or do you want to escape you current situation?

A dream of a spinning globe can indicate you feel your world spinning out of control. Holding a globe in your hands suggests you feel fully in control of your own world.

Archaeologist

Archaeologists delve into the past, aiming to piece together a slice of history, sometimes from tiny fragments. The profession can range from digging up fossilized bone in some of the hottest landscapes in the world to poring over ancient papyri and deciphering the contents of prehistoric burial mounds. While not the most glamorous of jobs, it is nevertheless essential in establishing how the world and the creatures on it, including ourselves, evolved.

In your dream: Are you 'digging up the past' for a particular reason, perhaps related to an old relationship or job? Does the dream reflect a desire to learn about yourself, your own history, where you came from? Or is it a wish to understand the wider world and your place within it?

Curator

Tending the artefacts of the past requires a steady hand and a knowledgeable mind.

In your dream: Dreaming of being a curator implies an interest in history and in learning, possibly for the sake of learning rather than for career advancement. Do you see yourself as being a caretaker, helping to preserve knowledge for future generations?

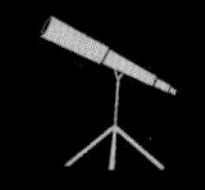

Librarian, web content manager

Librarians and webmasters are custodians of knowledge, keeping their collections well-ordered so that others may access information easily and speedily.

In your dream: Dreaming of doing such a job suggests that you may be frustrated in your personal search for knowledge or information in waking life, or that you feel capable of taking on this sort of work.

NUMBERS

Unless you work with numbers as an accountant or teacher, for example, dreams that focus specifically on numbers are fairly unusual and therefore significant. They may indicate important dates, anniversaries or ages, or represent a countdown of some kind. Numbers have carried symbolic meanings throughout history; you may, for instance, be familiar with the magpie counting rhyme:

One for sorrow
Two for joy
Three for a girl
Four for a boy
Five for silver
Six for gold
Seven for a secret never to be told.

Remember, though, that meanings vary from culture to culture. The most common meanings of the numbers are listed here but you will need to interpret them according to other elements of the dream and the significance a number carries for you.

In your dream: What did the numbers refer to? Dates, house numbers map references, people? Were you counting numbers, or looking for a specific number? If you dreamed of a countdown, was it to something good or bad?

Zero

Void, nothingness, infinity, limitless possibility. In the Tarot, the Fool – complete spontaneity, originality, eccentricity.

One

Starting point, the self, solitude, unity, perfection, maleness, God, the Primum Mobile (the force behind the form, the creator). In astrology, the Sun. In the Tarot, the Magician – determination, initiative, control.

Two

Duality (good and evil, dark and light), polarity, company, femaleness, second place. The interaction of male and female, symmetry and balance, strife. In astrology, the Moon. In the Tarot, the High Priestess – inner power, meditation, reflection.

Three

The trinity, the triangle. Mind, body and spirit, the mother, father and child, good luck. In the Tarot, the Empress – fertility, the mother and motherhood, security.

Four

The elements (air, earth, fire and water), the seasons, cardinal points of the compass, harmony and stability. The square. Protection. In the East, four is unlucky: in some languages the word for 'four' sounds the same as the word for 'die'. In the Tarot, the Emperor – the father, authority, discipline, courage.

Five

The five senses, the fingers that make us tool-users and creators. Five is a lucky number in the Orient. In the Tarot, the High Priest – integrity, honesty, belief.

Six

Traditionally sensuality, harmony, beauty, tactfulness, perfection. In the Tarot, the Lovers – passion, devotion, love.

Seven

The days of the week. Traditionally seven symbolizes mystery and is considered a very magical number. In the Tarot, the Chariot – change, transformation.

Eight

Traditionally the number of regeneration. In the Tarot, Justice – truth, conscience, balance.

Nine

Eternity. The Moon, dreams, illusion. In the Tarot, the Hermit – solitude, searching, wisdom.

In your dream: Were you struggling with mathematical formulae, trying to solve a complex problem or effortlessly performing complicated arithmetic? How does this relate to your waking life?

Ten

Traditionally the Law. In the Tarot, the Wheel of Fortune – innovation, fluctuation, opportunity.

Eleven

Lacking its own particular commonplace meaning, this stands for any largish but non-specific number. In the Tarot, Strength.

Twelve

Traditionally the number of spiritual order, the signs of the zodiac. In the Tarot, the Hanged Man – submission, sacrifice, perseverance.

Thirteen

Considered unlucky for centuries, partly because it symbolizes death and rebirth. In the Tarot, Death – challenge, the possibility of failure, conclusion.

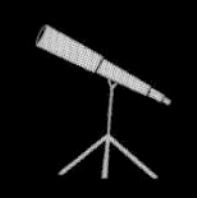

SHAPES

All our world is made of shapes and for a shape to be significant in a dream it needs to stand out in some way. You may dream of a cube or triangle floating in space, but dreams are more commonly filled with recognizable entities rather than abstracts, so take note of any shape that draws attention to itself – a circular house, for example, or a person made up of box-shapes.

In your dream: Numbers and shapes are often intricately interlinked in dreams – sometimes in a contradictory way. A dream of a seven-sided triangle, for example, or a four-sided circle, may be urging you to step back and look at life from an entirely new perspective.

Circle, oval, egg-shape

Circular shapes represent infinite possibility – the womb, the expanding universe, the planet with all its diversity and potential. Unless the circle is broken, dreams where this shape predominates are positive and symbolize steady growth and progress.

(See also Mandala, page 359)

Triangle

The upward triangle represents aspiration ascending from a firm foundation; the downward triangle represents a delving into your own subconscious mind to explore yourself. The two combined – one laid over the other – make a six-pointed star and symbolize the whole person, mind, body and spirit in harmony.

Pointing to the side, a triangle can indicate the direction you should follow.

Square, rectangle

The sturdy square is the basis of most buildings. The square and the more elongated rectangle represent strength and stability, in dreams as in waking life.

Column

Are you putting someone on a pedestal? Is someone doing this to you? Bear in mind it can be a long way to fall.

Spiral

The spiral is a dynamic shape. Winding outwards, it represents growth, expansion, development. Winding inwards, it symbolizes focus, a reduction to the simplest, death in order to effect transformation.

In your dream: Does the shape represent you? Are you a square, stable and perhaps a little stolid? Or are you flexible and complex like the spiral? Did you appear in your dream more as an hourglass – and did that represent your physical body or time passing?

Möbius strip

The Möbius strip – best envisaged as a strip of paper given a half-twist and the ends glued to make a shape with a never-ending single surface - represents infinity. It can indicate that you feel you're on a never-ending trip or task.

Other shapes

A **cone** may represent a megaphone, suggesting you need to speak out about something or, if you associate it with a black hole, irreversible change.

The significance of **unusual or bizarre shapes** depends almost entirely on the dreamer: you will need to consider what the shape reminds you of in order to gain some insight into its meaning.

TIME

Time in dreams doesn't work in the same way as it does in our waking lives: aeons can pass in a single dream or time can stand still; often, time passing in the way we understand it when we are awake has no meaning or impact in dreams. Awareness of a certain time of day or era can be symbolic of a stage of life or hold clues to the other images or events in a dream.

In your dream: A focus on time or its passing, or on clocks or other timepieces, can indicate worry that time is passing too quickly, or that you have not had enough time to allow you to complete an important task. It may also symbolize a fear of growing old.

Past

A dream set in the past can indicate the memory of a real event, nostalgia for your own past or a wish to go back to an earlier or more simple time, perhaps because something about the period intrigues you in waking life.

Future

Dreaming of the future often expresses a hope for a utopian cure for all the ills of the modern world, but it may represent a short-cut, a wish to get there without it having to be worked for by the current generation.

Morning

A dream set in the morning often indicates the start of a project or relationship.

Afternoon

If it's afternoon in the dream, are you preparing to finish something – an occupation, for example – or are you looking forwards to leaving work to have some fun? If you're approaching **retirement** this dream may become more prevalent: consider the other elements of the dream to see if they give any suggestions of an appropriate and enjoyable way to spend the time.

Day

If it's daylight in the dream, the events will represent normal daily life, events that your subconscious feels **should** happen in daylight.

Night

A dream of night-time events may simply symbolize events that normally happen at night. However, it can also suggest the clandestine or illicit, things that you would normally wish to be hidden away from the public gaze – a meeting with a lover, for example, or a burglary or a conspiracy.

Being late, being early

Dreaming of such things is likely to reflect a fear of doing the same in waking life. Falling behind or being late may mean missing opportunities, as can **missing appointments** or failing to attend an interview.

Being early, on the other hand, usually indicates that you are comfortably in control of the events in your life.

In waking life: We are all subject to the demands of passing time – the need to do certain things at certain times, the biological clock moving inexorably onwards, the body aging as the years pass. To dream of such things may be your subconscious suggesting you take steps to fulfil your dreams and ambitions before it's too late.

Clock, watch

Dreams prominently featuring a timepiece imply an awareness of time passing, perhaps of time being wasted, especially if you found the ticking of the clock sinister.

Time travel

To dream of time travel suggests that you aren't happy in your own time. Travelling to the past indicates you believe you'd be happier in a less sophisticated world with a slower pace of life, while travelling forwards in time suggests a forward-looking and intensely curious mind.

Dreaming of time travel to **right wrongs** or **prevent disasters** suggests a noble and compassionate mind frustrated with its inability to change current events.

THE ARTS

A dream of being involved in the arts is often expressing the creative side of your character.

Painting, sculpture, photograph

These visual works of art essentially provide a 'snapshot' of a moment in time.

In your dream: What did the artwork depict? A living creature or a landscape? A portrait or an abstract? To decipher the meaning, check the subject meaning in other sections of this book.
(See also Art Gallery page 308)

Artist, photographer

A dream of being an artist is generally your subconscious expressing a straightforward wish for you to fulfil your artistic abilities in some form.

In your dream: Were you drawing, painting or photographing? Or working in a more tactile medium, perhaps sculpting, using sensuous textiles or shaping clay? Are you more comfortable and accomplished with three-dimensional art or do you prefer working in two? Have you ever tried the variety of art in the dream? Consider giving it a try; you might be very pleasantly surprised.

A **book illustrator** can open up 'a world of wonder' to the reader, but book illustrations can also impose one vision of the work, rather than encouraging readers' own imagination. To some extent, dreaming of book illustrating suggests you want to be in control of how people see you and your work.

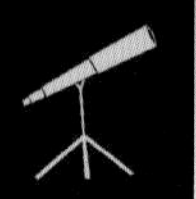

Musician

Music is an ancient art form and one that appeals intimately to the emotions. There's a huge variety of musical types, each with its own practitioners and fans, and each with its own emotional impact.

In your dream: Were you **writing music**, **conducting an orchestra**, **playing an instrument**, **singing**? In waking life, would you rather take a vital but background role, be the controlling force, play as part of a team or be in the spotlight? What sort of music was involved and how do you feel about it in waking life? If it was something you don't usually enjoy, what was it trying to tell you? That you might benefit from the discipline and complexity of classical music? Or that paying some attention to today's music could enliven your mind, help you break out of a rut, enable you to communicate more effectively?

It might be that your subconscious is suggesting the possibility of 'making sweet music' with a partner or group, stressing the benefits of cooperation, especially if you weren't singing or playing in tune. If the music was off-key in the dream, it's quite likely that something is also off-key in your waking life.

Musical instruments

Dreaming of playing a musical instrument suggests a wish to appeal to the emotions of others: the type of music and instrument reveals which emotional state you may be trying to summon.

In your dream: Which instrument featured? Most stringed instruments are, for their rounded shape as much as for their sound, considered feminine. The **cello** and **guitar** in particular are often seen as representing the female body. The **harp** is romantic and wistful, very feminine.

Brass instruments, on the other hand, are loud, brash and challenging. Have you been 'blowing your own trumpet' recently? How was the sound received by the dream audience?

Wind instruments are phallic in shape, but their sound is soft and gentle, almost wooing. A dream of playing a **flute** or **oboe** suggests a wish to persuade and cajole rather than use force.

The **piano**, **organ** and **synthesizer** are versatile and powerful, used for a wide variety of musical types. Dreaming of playing them well suggests self-confidence in most areas of your life.

Drums, **cymbals** and other percussion instruments can symbolize 'marching to the beat of a different drum', especially if you are independent and strongly individual in waking life. They are also loud and rousing: are you trying to attract attention?

Cameraman, film crew

Being behind the lens makes you an acute observer, but also gives you power over what is seen.

In your waking life: Do you view life as a film, with yourself an observer rather than a participant? Or would you like to control what you experience, remove the unpleasant and only see the beautiful?

Designer

The occupation of designer can cover a multitude of things from fabrics, furniture and the home as a whole, to clothes, cars or other machinery.

In your dream: What were you designing? Was it for yourself or others? Do you have a subconscious wish to order the lives of other people? Do you consider yourself more 'tasteful' than the people you were working for – and did you think them inferior because of it? Does this apply to your real occupation as well?

Language

Language is a powerful tool of communication. In dreams it is not uncommon to be able to understand languages, even made up ones, that we cannot speak in our waking lives.

In your dream: Did you recognize the language or remember any of the words or were you left completely baffled? Are you having communication problems in waking life or is someone speaking 'gobbledegook' to you, making no sense but still expecting you to follow orders?
(See also Countries and Continents, page 32)

Writer

Writing, like the visual arts, is a way of expressing yourself; it is also an effective form of communication, used to explain your views to a wider audience. Dreaming of writing a book often suggests that you have something you want to tell the world, a story or perhaps an idea, especially if the dream is recurrent.

In your dream: What were you writing? A play for other people to act out or entertaining fiction? Poetry to appeal to the emotions or a book or article expressing your views? Or the script for an epic new film? In this instance it would be beneficial to take a lead from the dream and try it. No one has to see the result if you don't want them to, and you may find you have previously unknown talent.

Books

Books convey information from the writer to the reader; they can instruct, guide, inspire and entertain. In the right or wrong hands they can even change the world. The significance of books in a dream is dependent on a number of considerations: the type of book, the surrounding landscape and your relationship with books as a whole – for example, being in a library surrounded by books may be heaven to a bibliophile, but a nightmare to someone who can't read!

In your dream: If your dream involved just one book or many, was it one you know or was it completely unfamiliar? If you couldn't tell what was in it, your subconscious may be suggesting that something is 'a closed book' to you, or that it's time to learn something new.

If there were many books, did you feel excited or overwhelmed? The latter wouldn't be unusual if you're anticipating some sort of test or examination, and might be your mind's way of telling you to study harder!

Were the books in a library, a shop or on your own shelves? Did you see books as things to be borrowed or owned and what does that tell you about your feelings for what they symbolize? **Discarded books** may represent a danger of discarding something important because it seems old or outmoded.

(See also Writer, page 253; Library, page 306)

COLOURS

People who are very aware of colour will usually dream in colour, while those who aren't may find their dreams are mostly in black and white. Occasionally, one or two colours will predominate and these dreams are worth examining in detail, noting what objects were coloured and how. Colours are often associated with particular emotions, so see also Emotions, page 130.

Yellow

Despite its sunny, cheerful hue, yellow has come to symbolize cowardice, deceit and irresponsibility.

In your dream: Is your subconscious warning you about someone seemingly friendly on the surface but working to undermine you, your work or a relationship? Or are you accusing yourself of cowardice, of not facing up to your responsibilities?

Orange

Warm and responsive, orange generally suggests optimism and cooperation.

In your dream: Does the colour add overtones of warmth or is it a bright, hard colour? Orange is close to gold in colour and in dreams may indicate an appreciation of life's riches.

Red

In the West, red is the colour of danger, passion and anger. In the East, it is considered a very lucky colour, used for weddings and holidays and for making gifts of money.

In your dream: Is your subconscious warning you of some threat in your waking life, an actual physical danger or because your finances are 'in the red'? Are you angry or is someone angry with you, so much that it colours your life? Or are you 'painting the town red' in celebration and perhaps overdoing it? If you have emotional ties to the East or there are oriental motifs in the dream, consider also the colour's Eastern symbolism.
[See also Blood, page 125]

Blue

In nature, blue is the most relaxing colour, but symbolically it can have a variety of different meanings. If we're depressed, we 'feel blue'; surprises or shocks arrive 'out of the blue', while 'into the blue' means into the unknown. Dark blue is a favoured colour for uniforms, suggesting people in authority or even oppression; 'true blue' indicates loyalty to a person or party; sky blue feels uplifting and blue is also lucky for a bride to carry – hence the 'something blue' in the traditional rhyme.

In your dream: Given the number of different associations, you will need to decide what blue means to you personally in order to decide its significance in the dream. Different shades of blue also mean different things – bright sky blue is uplifting and enlivening, while dark blue is depressing.

Green

The colour of nature, of growing things and hence symbolic of fertility – individuals who have unusual success in growing plants are said to have 'green fingers' or 'a green thumb'. Green is also soothing and calming. However, green is also associated with jealousy. Dreams may also be tinted green if you are 'green' yourself – starting a new job, for example or entering into a relationship for the first time.

In your dream: A predominance of green may indicate a particular appreciation of the environment and the need to care for it, especially if the dream took place in a natural, outdoor setting.

Alternatively, it may indicate envy. Depending on who or what was in the dream, ask yourself if you are envious of someone or if someone is jealous of you and why.
(See also Jealousy, page 133; Gardener, page 174)

Purple

Purple has always been associated with royalty, originally because the difficulty of creating the dye made it extremely expensive. Depending on the depth of colour, it may also seem gloomy.

In your dream: A predominance of purple may suggest that you feel distanced from those around you, finding it difficult to find common ground or communicate easily.

Black

In the West, black is often seen as symbolic of death and mourning, and dark or hidden 'occult' things. Less sombrely, it also has associations with formality and sophistication, as seen in a 'black-tie' event, and often the chosen clothing colour for religious or academic people.

In your dream: The significance of black depends to a large extent on the feelings and circumstances associated with the dream, but it's usually indicative of a potential problem and should be considered seriously. If your subconscious is showing you such a dark aspect of yourself, and especially if it's frequent or recurring, it might be wise to seek some sort of counselling. Are you depressed? Feeling lost or confused? Searching for someone or something to provide you with an anchor? Are you being 'kept in the dark' in your waking life?

If you were specifically dressing in black, are you anticipating some sort of ceremony? A graduation, perhaps, or an important business function – a business that's 'in the black' is doing well. Alternatively, it's not unusual to dream a lot of black if you have recently suffered a death in the family – it represents your grief and is a symbol of mourning.
(See also Sorrow, page 132; Loss, page 164)

White

In the West, white most often symbolizes innocence and purity, and bridal white is frequently worn by a woman on her wedding day. In dreams white often indicates that you are starting afresh, and is an optimistic image. In the East, however, white is the colour of death and mourning.

In your dream: Did white add a feeling of freshness and newness? Or was it presenting a tabula rasa – a clean slate on which nothing is yet written? Do you feel you would like to start afresh or that you are a 'blank page' awaiting words?

White also has connotations of 'whitewash', covering up unpleasantness or corruption by painting over it. If this is the significance in your own dream, it might be sensible to consider whether continuing is worth the possible cost.
[See also Wedding, page 365]

10 DAILY LIFE

The expression 'enough to feed and clothe yourself and a roof over your head' is often used to sum up the basic physical needs in life. This chapter includes cream cakes and diamond rings as well as the basics because our dreams are full of wish-fulfilment and fantasy. Certain foods and articles of clothing also carry with them connotations far removed from keeping us warm and fed.

FOOD AND DRINK

Dreaming of a particular food may just be your subconscious indicating a lack in your diet (such as strawberries representing vitamin C), so consider all possibilities before deciding which is most appropriate.

Meal

Meals bring us together and suggest conviviality and sharing. They can range from a formal dinner, when manners and dress need to be appropriate, to a snack or coffee and a chat with a friend.

In your dream: What type of meal was it? A **picnic** is relaxed and informal and usually takes place in warm, balmy weather: if you find yourself having a picnic in the rain, it may suggest a spell of depression. A **family dinner** can be either a happy, laughing occasion or a source of much embarrassment and unhappiness, depending on your feelings for your family. An **intimate meal** with a mate or lover, a **boys' night in** watching the TV with beer? Important things to note are who you are eating and drinking **with** (they may be very important to you, even if you aren't yet close), where the meal is taking place, and most importantly, how you feel about the event.
(See also Taste page 127)

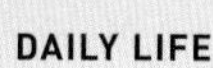

Bread

Bread in all its multitudinous forms is such a staple food it's difficult to imagine being without it. Every culture has a version, from pitta to naan, focaccia to anpan, bagel to sourdough, the list is almost endless. Bread can be eaten for every meal, toasted, fried or filled. It can even be imbued with religious meaning: it is a vital part of the Christian Communion, and the ancient Greeks formed bread into a crescent moon for Artemis and an egg shape to represent the fertilizing powers of Demeter. Bread nourishes not only our body, but also our feelings, acting as a simple but satisfying 'comfort food'.

In your dream: Bread serves the same purpose as it does in our waking lives and can act as a 'grounding' aspect. If you see it as a convenience food, it will represent just that – so if you find yourself serving roughly made sandwiches at a posh dinner party, your subconscious is probably pointing out that you need to pay a little more attention to the niceties of life!

Bread may also symbolize money, 'dough', in dreams: accepting from or offering it to others suggests the exchange of cash.

(See also Communion Bread and Wine, page 355)

Apple

Apples have been considered a magical fruit for millennia, but they also symbolize health, a wholesome lifestyle and a loving, nurturing home ('homely as apple pie').

In your dream: Giving or receiving an apple can indicate a wish for a sound, healthy, pragmatic relationship, based on and around the family, rather than a passionate sexual affair.

It's possible that a dream apple may represent temptation. Did you accept the apple, give in to the lure? Or were you strong and resisted the enticement?

(See also Apple tree, page 49)

Melons

Melons primarily symbolize women's breasts, although they are also wonderfully delicious, sweet and juicy treats.

In your dream: Eating a melon may just be reliving a pleasant recent memory of eating the fruit, but it's another lovers' choice and could reflect enjoyable lovemaking.

(See also Breast, page 120)

Figs

Many fruits are seen as sexual symbols, either because of their shape and colour, or their reputation. Figs, for example, often represent the female genitalia in art and can do the same in dreams.

In your dream: Eating or offering figs in a dream is most likely a straightforward symbol of physical attraction or the wish for some intimate activity.

Lemon

Lemons are an essential ingredient in many recipes and medicines – the high vitamin C content makes them good for health – but they are extremely acidic, not the sort of fruit that's comfortable or comforting to eat by itself.

In your dream: Eating lemons may suggest you're finding something in your waking life very sour, difficult to stomach. Do other elements of the dream give any indication as to what it is; can you add a 'spoonful of sugar' to help make the situation more palatable?

Strawberry

Strawberries are considered an aphrodisiac, as much for their heart shape as for their bright red hue, the colour of passion. The fact that they taste deliciously sweet and have a wonderful fragrance doesn't hurt either.

In your dream: Who are you eating strawberries with? Are you feeding each other? A dream of eating strawberries out of season may indicate a dream fulfilled or about to be.

Orange

Because of their shape and colour, and the fact that they grow in hot climates, oranges often symbolize the sun, warmth and growth in dreams.

In your dream: Eating an orange in an otherwise gloomy atmosphere suggests that your subconscious is reassuring you that no matter how grim things seem right now, there is light on the horizon. The giving or receiving of an orange may be saying 'you are the sunshine of my life'.

Banana

A banana represents the penis.

In your dream: Eating a banana has unsubtle sexual connotations. In contrast, mashing, cutting or puréeing a banana in a dream suggests a degree of anger or frustration towards a male in your life.

Grape

Grapes have a reputation for being a slightly decadent fruit, partly because it takes a lot of heat and sunshine to ripen them properly, and also because they are made into wine.

In your dream: Feeding someone or being fed grapes symbolizes sensual luxury and a relaxed attitude towards sex. It is also suggestive of Roman orgies.

Pear

The shape of a pear, rather like an apple that has sagged, has led to it being used to express something that has slumped: a project that has gone 'pear-shaped'; a woman with a pear-shaped body.

In your dream: A pear may indicate a subconscious awareness that elements of your life are less than ideal – that a particular aspect has 'gone pear-shaped'. Alternatively your mind may be making a pun on 'pair', but only you can decide the significance of that!

Peach

With their velvety skin and rounded shape, peaches are another sexual symbol.

In your dream: People with a liking for buttocks may find themselves dreaming of this fruit.

Coconut

Round and full of milk, coconuts are an obvious symbol of the female breast.

In your dream: Unlike melons or other soft, juicy fruit that suggest breasts, coconuts have a very tough outer casing and grow out of easy reach – you have to work hard to be rewarded by their milk and sweet flesh. Does this help interpret other parts of your dream, or an aspect of your waking life?
(See also Breast, page 120)

Nut

Nuts of all varieties generally symbolize testicles.

In your dream: Cracking nuts open suggests a wish to humiliate a man, probably someone who has annoyed or embarrassed you.

Tomato

Tomatoes were once known as 'love apples' and considered an aphrodisiac, mostly due to the bright red colour and the fact that they are full of tiny seeds. Interestingly, there are indications that eating tomatoes may help prevent male-specific diseases like prostate cancer.

In your dream: Tomatoes in dreams may indicate a healthy sex life.

Carrot

Carrots are a fairly obvious phallic symbol, as are cucumbers, leeks and marrows of different types and sizes.

In your dream: Their appearance in dreams suggest that sexual matters are of considerable significance in your life at the moment, though the meaning will depend on the situation and circumstances in which the vegetables appear. Eating them eagerly may indicate a voracious sexual appetite, but if they are small and stunted you're most likely to be feeling either frustrated (if you're female) or insecure and inferior (if you're male).
(See also Groin, page 121)

Corn

Corn, especially on the cob, can symbolize the male genitals in dreams.

In your dream: Sweetcorn's cheerful yellow colour and sweet taste are appealing and suggest a playful, happy appreciation of sex.

Onions

Onions are noted for their distinctive and flavourful smell and taste, their antiseptic and disease-combating qualities and their multiple skins or layers. Metaphorically they have come to symbolize the layers of the human mind, from the surface thoughts through the memories and down into the subconscious (in Jungian terms the Id, Ego and Super-ego).

In your dream: Dreaming of onions, especially if you're peeling them, may indicate a wish to get to the bottom of someone's psyche, find out what makes them tick. Or perhaps you feel like crying and wish to blame it on something outside yourself.

Potato

Along with other root vegetables like swede or turnip, potatoes are a basic, filling and very versatile food, but have also come to symbolize someone who is ignorant or unintelligent, 'a bit thick', in other words.

In your dream: Do the potatoes represent someone in particular – a 'couch potato', perhaps? Or are you on a diet and craving the naughtiness of French fries?

Meat

A source of concentrated protein, meats of various kinds have formed the main element of many human meals from earliest times.

In your dream: A dream of eating meat may indicate an urge to get in touch with your more primitive side, especially if you're vegetarian in waking life.

Seafood

Cooked seafood's smell and pink flesh most often represent the female sex organs in dreams: eating seafood is a fairly straightforward sexual symbol. Alternatively, there may be a subconscious link between seafood and the sea. The ocean exerts a fascination over most people, which may express itself in this way.

In your dream: Were you eating the seafood or might it have been a link with the sea that was a feature of the dream?

Oysters are considered an aphrodisiac – a dream of eating them suggests your sex life might need a little stimulation. (See also Sea, page 29; Merfolk, page 374)

Herbs

Herbs have medicinal and practical as well as culinary uses, and some have particular symbolism: rosemary for remembrance; rue for regret, for example.

In your dream: Did a single herb have particular prominence? Rosemary may suggest you've forgotten something important, while **sage** in dreams is usually a pun on wisdom.

Mint is cleansing and freshening, which is why it's used in so many cleaning preparations like toothpaste. In a dream it may suggest that some aspect of your life needs cleaning. **Parsley** cancels out the strong smell of garlic, so may indicate that something is being covered up. **Thyme**'s appearance may simply be a pun on time, and whether you're making the best use of time - or wasting it.

Salt

Salt is the basic food seasoning, once considered so valuable that workers were paid in salt. However, too much can be very unhealthy.

In your dream: Was there too much or too little salt in the dream? Are you eating healthily in waking life? Or does someone think you 'aren't worth your salt'?

Pepper

Once rare and valuable, pepper adds heat to food.

In your dream: Dreams of grinding pepper on to a meal suggests you feel the need for some extra excitement in your waking life.

Spices

Spices are generally used to add interest and heat to dishes, and dreaming of specific spices may indicate the need to do the same in your waking life.

In your dream: Ginger is hot, spicy and an aid to digestion, and so it may suggest a need to 'ginger up' your waking life, try something new and daring. The **curry spices**, cardamom, cumin, turmeric and the like, may suggest you're trying to 'curry favour' with someone. **Chilli** may indicate a hot, fiery nature in need of cooling down.

Chocolate

Chocolate occupies a special niche. In chemical terms it's a very complex foodstuff, causing a variety of pleasant reactions in the body (with the exception of those people who are allergic to it), almost like being in love. The name of the plant from which it comes translates as 'food of the gods', and there are vast numbers of people who would agree wholeheartedly!

In your dream: Were you eating chocolate by yourself? With others? Were you giving it or was it being given to you? Chocolate is a favourite gift for lovers to give to each other, a symbol of affection. Too much, however, can cause weight-gain: did you feel guilty eating it? Are you in love or was the chocolate acting as a substitute for romance?

Cakes and pastries

These come in a host of different shapes and sizes. The significance of the cake depends a great deal on what it suggests to you in waking life. If you usually avoid cakes but were eating them in the dream, perhaps you need to allow yourself some sweet treats in waking life.

In your dream: Were you enjoying a **birthday cake**, with candles and the accompanying presents or a rich, fruity winter season cake while the snow fell outside? **Apple pie** with cream, redolent of the comforts of home? Or was it a **cheesecake**, a delicious treat? Were you struggling to eat a **rock cake** that threatened to break your teeth or a **meringue**, light and sweet but with no substance to it? Were you looking through a window at the delicacies on display but unable to get to them? Maybe you feel you're being denied the sweet things of life.

Ice cream

Something of an ephemeral luxury, as once out of the freezer ice cream rapidly melts.

In your dream: Eating ice cream may be a warning from your subconscious to 'cool down' a relationship, especially if you were sharing the ice cream with another person.

Snacks and sweets

Peanuts, crisps, chocolate bars and other snacks might be viewed as treats, rewards, 'something to keep me going' or a quick-fix form of solace. They often assume greater importance if we are denied them and may be associated with guilty pleasure.

In your dream: Recurring images always deserve a closer examination. If you find yourself dream-snacking frequently, your subconscious might be warning you that you're eating unhealthily or that there's something in the snack that your body needs. It would be sensible to check further into the matter, in any case.

Drugs

Drugs modify our bodily chemical or physical processes, usually only temporarily, although all drugs have the potential to cause irreparable damage. Most can be addictive, some more so than others. Many are used for medical purposes. Others, so-called recreational drugs, span a wide range from marijuana through designer drugs such as Ecstasy and LSD to highly addictive heroin and cocaine; these are often illegal. Some, like tobacco, caffeine and alcohol, are used so regularly that the fact that they *are* drugs is forgotten.

In your dream: If you were taking **medical drugs**, can you determine why? Are you on a course of medication and concerned about side-effects or efficacy? If you're worried about a possible illnesses it would be sensible to see a health professional.

Or were you taking a **recreational drug**? What was the effect? Why did you take it – to escape stress or boredom or hostility in your waking life? To try something new and illicit? As a gesture of rebellion? These last two are more likely if you are generally law-abiding in waking life. Consider other, legal and less dangerous ways of 'getting high'!

Tobacco is both addictive and carries unpleasant health risks, including cancer. If you are a smoker and dreamed about smoking, what was the context? Were you alone, with other smokers or were non-smokers glaring at you for polluting their air? Is your subconscious suggesting you give up, or are you determinedly continuing with the habit? (See also Coffee, page 280; Alcohol, page 281)

Water

Water is one of life's absolute essentials; we can survive much longer without food than we can without water.

In your dream: Dreaming of drinking a lot of water suggests you are feeling 'dry', of ideas, of feelings, of emotions, especially if you can't slake your thirst.

Egg

Eggs are almost magical things, little wombs that contain the potential for new life.

In your dream: Eating eggs may indicate a wish to ingest new experiences or possibly a yearning for a child of your own. Breaking eggs may indicate a loss of hope, or alternatively making sacrifices in order to improve your life or that of others.

Milk

This is another basic food, one that newborn babies live on for the first months of life.

In your dream: Drinking milk can indicate a yearning to return to a state of babyhood, where someone else handles all the problems of life. The dream may occur when you're under particular stress.
(See also Breast, page 120)

Butter

Butter is used to enrich foods, spread on bread or as a base for sauces.

In your dream: A dream focusing on butter may indicate a need for something – possibly money – to make your waking life more palatable. Was it spread on bread, which can also symbolize 'dough' or money?

Tea

Despite being a mild stimulant, tea is usually drunk as an aid to relaxation. Taking tea can also be a ritual, from a regular afternoon pause to a formal ceremony.

In your dream: Dreaming of a formal tea party or a tea ritual may indicate your need to relax but within a particular setting – a formal, all-inclusive holiday, for example, or structured classes in a new subject.

Coffee

The caffeine in coffee is a stimulant, useful for jolting the mind and body awake, especially in the morning.

In your dream: A dream of coffee or other **caffeine drinks** is unlikely to have any great significance unless you avoid caffeine in waking life. In this instance, how did you feel about it? Are you under pressure to conform? Or are you searching for something to help you to perform better? Dreaming of coffee, whether you usually drink it or not, may indicate you feel you aren't performing to your best ability and need some external stimulus.

Alcohol

Alcoholic drinks are usually drunk for their taste and effect, that of loosening inhibitions and relaxing the body. Different drinks have their own associations relating to class and gender stereotypes.

Beer, ale or **cider** are usually perceived as basic, honest and hearty, drunk by hard-working manual labourers. **Wine** is a more sophisticated beverage, often associated with the academic or intellectual sphere. **Scotch** is seen as bluff, sturdy and hot-tempered, **vodka** as dour, even grim, and relentless, **brandy** as expansive and genial, and **rum** as exotic and well-travelled. **Gin** has more of a status stereotype, gin and tonic being seen as the favoured drink of the upper classes. **Liqueurs**, sweet and strong, are often perceived as a woman's drink, while **cocktails** are exotic and fun, very much party fare.

In your dream: What sort of alcohol are you drinking? What are the circumstances and how are you feeling? Are you drinking alone and if so, why? Perhaps your subconscious is advising you not to become introspective, to stay in touch with others.

If you are socializing, consider what the dream is suggesting. Should you 'loosen up' when you're with friends, be a little more open about yourself? Or is it a warning that you are **too** unguarded and honest in your dealings with others and need to be a little more restrained?

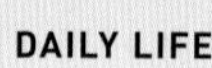

Fruit juice

Fruit juice is almost the opposite of alcohol, refreshing, enlivening and healthy.

In your dream: Drinking fruit juice may indicate a warning to take care of your health.

Carbonated drinks

Drinks with a fizz usually indicate a light, playful, sparkling personality or occasion, or the need to lighten the atmosphere.

In your dream: Where were you in the dream? Are you finding work or home life dull or tedious? Is there any way you can make it more interesting?

CLOTHES

Clothing is often an outward expression of how we wish to be seen by others, and can indicate status, whether actual or apparent. Dressing casually in a dream when you normally wear smart clothes suggests an unrealized desire to relax a little, take some time away from the constraints of waking life. Uncharacteristically fine or flamboyant dream attire may reflect a subconscious wish to be noticed or admired.

Tie

Ties indicate a degree of formality and can be a form of badge: the club tie or the old school tie. They are also a form of ligature around the neck that could be restrictive.

In your dream: Is something strangling you in waking life? Are you being forced to 'wear' something at work that you feel is inappropriate or destined to fail, but are unable to speak out about – possibly because it's your superior's project?

Bowties are notoriously difficult to tie: a dream of struggling with one suggests you feel ill-equipped to handle formal occasions, from interviews to presentations.

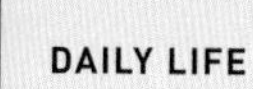

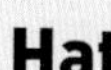

Hat

A practical hat offers protection from the elements, but hats can also be part of a uniform or the topping touch to dressing up on a formal or celebratory occasion.

In your dream: If you don't usually wear a hat in waking life, in dreams the image may be advising you to 'keep it under your hat' – your subconscious advising you to make sure you keep any secrets with which you're entrusted.

Shoes

Shoes can ease our walking or make it more difficult. We mould our shoes to our own very personal shape and talk about 'as comfortable as an old pair of shoes'. To 'walk around in someone else's shoes' is to get to see things from their point of view.

In your dream: Wearing uncomfortably **high-heeled, strappy or constricting shoes** may suggest that you feel 'hobbled' in waking life, perhaps by other people's expectations of how you should live. For a man to dream of someone else wearing such shoes can indicate a view of the other as prey – it's impossible to run far in such shoes – or as a helpless creature needing assistance. There's an obvious sexual element: the other is to a large extent at the man's mercy.

Trainers or sneakers indicate a desire to run away from a situation or person in waking life. What else were you wearing? If you were dressed for your wedding, it might be prudent to think twice about the commitment!

Heavy **working boots** suggest a period of hard, possibly physical work in the immediate future.

Laces

Shoe laces keep our shoes secure. If they come unravelled we may trip over our own feet.

In your dream: Untied laces may indicate that you are being careless in waking life, and are in danger or tripping yourself up if you aren't careful. A dream of **tying laces** suggests that you are preparing yourself for action, forging ahead determinedly.

Gloves

Gloves can offer welcome protection from both the cold and from getting our hands dirty or hurt. They also have a suggestion of gentility and care: handling some 'with kid gloves' involves dealing cautiously with them, but you can also have 'an iron fist hidden in a velvet glove'.

In your dream: Are you trying to handle someone carefully in a delicate situation? Are you wearing gloves to keep your hands clean because you're involved in something dirty or distasteful? Or are you handling something dangerous, and if so, what? Perhaps you are in an explosive or volatile relationship or is someone at work 'spitting acid'?

Did you need to keep your hands warm in the dream because you're dealing with something or someone who leaves you cold?

If you're wearing **boxing gloves**, is it because you're ready for a fight or because you feel too clumsy or ham-fisted to deal with what is happening in your life at the moment?

Underwear

Underwear can be modesty's last defence or a frivolous or sensual sexual statement.

In your dream: Being happy just wearing underwear suggests that you feel confident about your own attractiveness, perhaps even a little too sure of yourself and your appeal. Such a dream frequently occurs in conjunction with sexual imagery, and may simply be an enjoyable fantasy. If you were embarrassed, however, are you worried about revealing too much of yourself to others? Or do you feel that you might be airing your dirty linen in public?

Evening dress

Dreaming of wearing an expensive outfit when you usually dress casually can indicate a hidden desire to be seen as someone, a person of wealth, taste and authority. If worn for a celebration or special occasion, it suggests an awareness that you need to look your best, or not let anyone down – especially if you're on a tight budget and the dream is accompanied by feelings of fear or anxiety.

In your dream: If you are planning to attend a formal occasion, a dream of wearing evening dress may simply be a mental rehearsal of the event. If you were dressed inappropriately, however – wearing a long chiffon dress or top hat and tails to a beach barbecue or visit to a farm – consider if you have been acting inadvisably in waking life. Are you giving yourself airs at work or in your social life? Do you feel that your job, partner, friends or lover are beneath you in some way? Is your subconscious warning you not to be a snob or avoid making yourself look ridiculous?

Wedding dress

Whether expensive or modest, a wedding celebrates a long-term commitment between two people, and generally involves something special to wear. White is a common colour for the bride's dress, especially for a first wedding: the colour in this instance may symbolize innocence and virginity, or a 'new page' in your life, starting out with a clean slate.

In your dream: The significance depends on what is happening in your waking life. Are you about to embark on a new phase of your life – an actual marriage, perhaps, or a long-term commitment to a new job or partner? If you were wearing a wedding outfit for no obvious reason, are you perhaps tired of your present circumstances and suppressing a wish to start anew?
(See also Wedding, page 365; White, page 259)

Graduation gown

Graduates usually wear a gown and sometimes a mortarboard on their head for their graduation ceremony, the proud culmination of several years of hard study at a college or university.

In your dream: Being dressed for a graduation ceremony suggests you feel you have achieved a long-term academic or intellectual goal, perhaps a course of study, although it may equally be a landmark achievement in your career or simply in life.

Dressing up, role-play

What you and other people wear in dreams can have considerable significance, especially if it's unusual or a form of disguise. A dream of wearing something you ordinarily would not wear can indicate a wish to hide, to camouflage yourself. Something exotic or designed to titillate sometimes indicates an anxiety that you aren't attractive, or feel the need for something extra to boost a relationship. Alternatively, dressing up may simply be a wish to let out a repressed, playful aspect of your nature!

In your dream: Were you dressing up for a party? In which case, did you have an ulterior motive, perhaps to feel less inhibited in approaching someone with a view to sex?

Were you involved in a drama, a play or film? Do you feel that you're 'acting a part' in your waking life?

Were you trying a new image, perhaps because your subconscious feels you should liven up how you appear to others? Perhaps it was to please a lover or partner, add some excitement to your sex life or to allow your usually hidden sense of fun or eccentricity out to play!

Wearing dull, **baggy clothing** may indicate a wish to be inconspicuous or to hide, or possibly the fear of appearing boring, depending on other elements of the dream.

(See also Nakedness, page 144; Actor, page 205)

Dressmaker, outfitter

Designing and making clothes, especially your own, may indicate a wish to take back control of your own life, at least on the surface, particularly if your place of work has a strict dress code.

In your waking life: Do you feel you have to dress in a particular way because of what you have been told is suitable or because of your age? Perhaps you should try stretching the boundaries, making and wearing something different and eccentric, even if only in private.

Spectacles, contact lenses

Wearing spectacles or lenses to help your sight is mainly of interest in dreams if you don't wear them in your waking life. Sunglasses have a different type of significance, as they offer protection, either from natural glare or others' stares.

In your dream: Spectacles may mean you are ignoring something that's right under your nose. Is your subconscious advising you to either have your eyes checked or to start looking more closely at the world around you?

Dreaming of contact lenses, especially tinted, can indicate a wish for a change of look, especially if you usually wear spectacles.

Dreaming of **not** wearing sunglasses to protect your eyes from the sun or the glare off snow or water suggests you have a careless attitude towards life. However, wearing them all the time indicates a wish to hide the emotions your eyes reveal. (See also Eyes, page 113; Sight, page 126)

Weaving, knitting, embroidery

Dreaming of using thread or wool to create something with your hands can be a complex symbol, especially if it's not something you do in waking life. The weaving or knitting of different colours and qualities of thread together frequently represents life – 'life's rich tapestry' filled with different experiences and people.

In your dream: Weaving or knitting vibrant fabric suggests you take exuberant joy in life; muted tones that life is less colourful. Embroidering something you already own indicates a wish for a change of style. Creating something as a gift for another indicates their importance to you.
(See also Colours, page 255)

Baby clothes

Baby clothes suggest a new life, either an actual child or a 'brain-child', a project on which many hopes are pinned.

In your dream: The type and colour of the clothes can offer further clues to the significance of the baby clothes (unless you or someone close to you is soon expecting a baby, in which case it may be just your subconscious rehearsing for the new arrival). Warm, engulfing clothes can suggest an anticipated spell of budget-tightening.
(See also Child, page 137; Birth, page 151)

JEWELLERY

In dreams the meaning of jewellery depends very much on where it is worn and what it is made of.
(See also Gems and Metals, page 64)

Crown

Crowns and tiaras have been symbols of royalty and nobility for millennia.

In your dream: Wearing a crown may indicate a wish to be seen as noble and worthy, a leader among people.

Earrings

Ear adornments – rings, studs, pendants, cuffs – naturally draw attention to the ears.

In your dream: Ear jewellery of any sort may indicate a warning to listen to others, and pay attention to what you're hearing.
(See also Ears, page 116)

Facial piercings

These still carry a hint of the rebel - studs through the eyebrow, lip or cheek are an obvious statement of the wish to stand out.

In your dream: Piercings may express an unconscious desire to be seen as different, unconventional, especially if you wouldn't 'dream' of having such piercings in your waking life. A dream of having a tongue piercing may be your subconscious warning you to be more aware of what you're saying – to bite or guard your tongue.

Neck jewellery

Necklaces of all kinds, from a fine chain to a heavy metal torc, draw attention to the throat and upper chest and are often an unconscious expression of the wearer's sexual nature, diverting the eyes to a woman's breasts or a man's chest. However, animal collars are also worn around the neck and used for restraint or control.

In your dream: Wearing a decorative chain or necklace of some sort may indicate a wish to be seen as more desirable, especially if you don't usually wear such articles.

Dreaming of wearing a **necklet** that's too heavy or attached to a **lead** may suggest a loss of control in your waking life or problems that are literally 'weighing you down'.

[See also Chest, Breast, page 120]

Arm jewellery

Arm bands, bracelets and **bangles** all draw attention to the arms, to display either muscle – the 'strong-arm' character – or slenderness and delicacy. Heavy, expensive arm jewellery also displays the wearer's wealth. But such symbols can also indicate subjugation (slaves' **fetters**, a criminal's **handcuffs**), and if the jewellery is so heavy you can't lift your hands your ability to take control of your own life is limited.

In your dream: Was the jewellery associated with wealth or beauty, or with restriction? Do you feel your hands are 'tied' in your waking life? Is this because someone else is restricting you or have you abdicated responsibility? Consider the circumstances surrounding the dream image before attempting any interpretation.
(See also Arms, page 119)

Leg jewellery

As with arm jewellery, leg adornments draw attention to the strength, or gracefulness, of the limb - or they may be a way to restrain the wearer, make it impossible for them to move speedily.

In your dream: If the leg ring was a shackle rather than an adornment, consider what may be holding you back in waking life. Do you feel you're hobbling along, unable to keep up? Does the dream help you to identify the cause of the problem?
(See also Arm Jewellery, above; Leg, page 122)

Body jewellery

Most body jewellery – nipple or genital piercing – is intended to only be seen by intimates. It's secretive, discreet, designed to enhance the erogenous zones, and surprise and hopefully delight the person who 'discovers' it on their partner's body. Decorations or weights may be hung from rings, or they can be used to restrain the wearer. The exception is a navel piercing, which is designed to be seen in public and draws attention to the stomach.

In your dream: Body piercings suggest a hidden, unconventionally erotic nature with a liking for 'naughty' secrets. There may also be an unconscious interest in the more unusual elements of sex-play: such piercings are painful until they heal.

Navel jewellery on a woman is often an unconscious expression of fertility and sexual maturity. In dreams, it may suggest an interest in having children.

Rings

Hands are expressive, powerful symbols of creativity and resourcefulness. Rings are status symbols, revealing the wearer's social, professional or financial position.

In your dream: Consider the type of ring, what it was made of, the circumstances surrounding it. Was it being given as a gift or to seal an agreement – like an **engagement ring**? Were the fingers covered with rings? If so the dream may be indicating the wearer is insecure and using wealth or ostentatious display to disguise their shortcomings.

Dreaming of wearing **toe rings** can be suggestive of a more exotic life.

(See also Hands, Fingers, pages 118–119)

11 BUILDINGS AND MAN-MADE STRUCTURES

Because much daily life takes place within buildings, the setting and state of one in a dream can be an important indicator of your perception of yourself and your position in life. Was it clean and comfortable? Were you at ease or not? If you were comfortable somewhere messy, your subconscious may be prompting you to do something unconventional or relax your standards a little in waking life! Or are you focusing too much on surface appearances and ignoring the deeper, more important elements of your life?

PARTS OF THE BUILDING

Door

Entrances and exits, when prominent in dreams, may symbolize you deliberately entering into a particular situation or relationship, depending on the sort or building it is. It may also be a symbolic reference to an opening in your own body. Whether you are using the door to enter or leave is also significant.

In your dream: What did the door lead to or from? An entrance into a tunnel or cave may have a sexual meaning, suggesting a straightforward desire for intimacy or it may indicate a wish to return to the womb, especially if you are stressed or depressed in waking life.

A door may also symbolize the mouth, and your ability to express yourself or not if the door is locked or obstructed.
(See also Mouth, page 114; Lock, page 300)

Window

Windows let light into a building. They also allow us both to see out and others to see in.

In your dream: Windows may indicate your sense of sight; peering in or out, trying not to be seen, can represent nosiness or spying on others.
(See also Eyes, page 113; Sight, page 126; Curtains, page 336)

Roof

A roof is protection from the elements, a shield from what life may rain down on us.

In your dream: The state of the roof may reflect the emotional effect others have on you. It is protection, but it may also be a barrier to rising higher.

Wall

Walls are the barriers that keep the world at bay. They mark out our own personal domain.

In your dream: Were the building's walls strong and sound, or falling to pieces? Think about other elements in your dream, as their soundness or otherwise may relate to your waking life in general or just one aspect of it.

Floor

The floor and below it, of course, the building's foundation, represent the basis upon which the whole structure is built.

In your dream: Did the floor or foundations reflect the state of the foundations of your own waking life? Was it sturdy and level, or broken and dangerous?

Stairs, steps, escalator, ladder

Stairs and steps symbolize a structured, disciplined way of ascending or descending from one place to another. In dreams, they usually represent both your current circumstances and how you are dealing with them.

In your dream: Climbing up indicates you are doing your best to achieve your goals and making progress, especially at work. **Climbing down** may mean that things are not going so well. Are you somehow undermining your own efforts?

A dream of ascending or descending on an escalator suggests you aren't completely in control of the situation. Trying to walk up a down escalator indicates you're struggling to change direction but feel you're making no progress.

Using a ladder suggests you are self-motivated, versatile and determined to achieve in all things.

Places from your past

We sometimes revisit places from our past in dreams – childhood home, old school or college, old holiday locations. Often this occurs at times when in the present we are feeling under stress.

In your dream: Did the place have a calming influence or was it somewhere you associated with fear and distress, turning the dream into something close to a nightmare? Consider the other elements – objects, other people, what you were doing, how you felt.

Was the place in a city, full of people and the bustle of daily life? By itself in a solitary landscape? In a village, accompanied by an intimate feeling of community? Were you comfortable with the location or did you feel threatened or isolated? How does this relate to your waking life?

Lock, bolt

Locks are ambiguous: they can be used to keep you or your property safe, or to confine you.

In your dream: Was the lock on your own property, keeping intruders out? If in the home of a friend or family member, are you unconsciously concerned about their safety?

A dream involving padlocks suggests anxiety about the security of your possessions. Have you had anything stolen in the past? Is your subconscious suggesting you ensure or insure the safety of your belongings?

Bolting a door may suggest you feel you're 'locking the stable door after the horse has bolted'. Have you allowed an opportunity to escape you?

Key

Keys in dreams are very significant. They can relate to locks and security (see opposite) or denote access to a restricted place (a heart? a mind?) or a way of decoding a message.

In your dream: Was the key large and old, small and modern, tiny and easily hidden, an electronic keypad? What did it represent? The 'key to your heart'? Security – a way of locking yourself away from harm, or locking something away so it can't hurt you? Were you being given the 'keys to the city' – your freedom, perhaps? Does it represent anger, a desire to lock something or someone up and 'throw away the key'?

Alternatively, was a person the key? Are you a key to another's life or well-being, or they to yours?

TYPES OF BUILDING

Home

Your home represents yourself, your body, mind and psyche. The size and state of your home in your dream is intimately connected to your perception of yourself and changes over time as you develop and learn. It may be influenced by how you are feeling at the time: if you're depressed, your home might appear dark and gloomy; illness may be reflected by a home full of sharp obstacles or being far too hot. If you feel under threat or scrutiny, you may dream of living in a glasshouse or a conservatory.

On another level, your home in dreams reflects both where you are now and where you want to be. If you like your home, and feel safe and comfortable there, your dream home will resemble it to a large extent even if the dream version is a tweaked image to make it more perfect!

In your dream: Were you happy there? If not, consider why. Did you feel threatened, or unhappy? What does the concept of 'home' mean to you? Was your childhood home happy and secure? If not, that may well be reflected in your dreams, either in nightmares or in wistful dreams of the ideal home – possibly with you being locked out or unable to reach it.

Bungalow

Such a single storey dwelling makes less efficient use of plot than a house, but is often more desirable for those who have problems climbing stairs.

In your dream: Why did you dream of a bungalow? Does it symbolize the secure family home of your childhood or do you prefer the idea of living closer to the ground?

House

Dreaming of acquiring a house if you don't have one expresses a desire to own property, to have 'your own place' that you can arrange and decorate to suit yourself. The fact that a house has two or more storeys, making efficient use of the plot on which it is built but necessitating effort to move from one floor to another, may also be significant.

In your dream: If you live in a single-storey home but dreamed of living in a house, is your subconscious telling you your mind is capable of far more than you believe? If you were in a large house, did you wander, looking in the rooms, or did you stay in one small area? The former suggests a willingness to explore, to at least taste new areas of life or fields of study, while the latter indicates you may be afraid of change, of the new, especially if you felt worried or afraid.

Flat, apartment

These homes are self-contained but give the security of people around you should you need help. On the other hand, they may be associated with noisy or hostile neighbours.

In your dream: Flats are often single-person homes. If you live in a house with others, are you subconsciously longing for a little freedom, a 'place of your own' where you can shut everyone else out?

Alternatively, are you experiencing 'information overload', trying to digest too much data in your daily life and your mind is asking for a break and a simpler setting?

Workplace

If you love your work, dreaming about it suggests you feel defined by what you do for a living. If you don't like your work, the dream may suggest you feel it's taken over your life. If you dream that you live at your workplace, it's probably time to take a holiday!

In your dream: Are you a 'wage slave' or never have time to enjoy what you've earned? If you dreamed of an unfamiliar workplace, are you telling yourself you'd like a change of job? Were you enjoying it or did you feel lost?

Shops

The type of shop represents an area of your life which needs attention; the significance of the dream depends on what sort of shop it was and how you feel about shopping in waking life.

In your dream: Was the dream very different from your waking life? If you like **clothes** shopping, for example, but find yourself shopping for **DIY** items, you probably won't enjoy the dream but it may be advising you that some basic repairs are necessary in your home or in your life, and to deal with those before concentrating on the surface decorating!

Market, auction

A cattle or livestock market may indicate you feel that you're being treated as nothing more than a piece of meat in waking life: are you perhaps being sexually harassed at work? An antiques auction suggests an appreciation of the value that comes with age.

In your dream: Lots of different stalls symbolizes freedom of choice, although not having the cash to pay for anything there can mean you feel 'on the outside looking in', or jealous or angry because your opportunity to choose is being denied.

Was the market prospering or dilapidated? If the latter, do you feel you're not finding the best choices possible in life? Or if despite appearances, you find something valuable there, perhaps your subconscious is implying that you shouldn't ignore an opportunity, person or place simply because it isn't clean and shiny!

Library

Libraries are places of quiet study and repositories of knowledge.

In your dream: Why were you there? To read in peace? To research a particular subject? To work? Is your subconscious telling you that you need to apply yourself in a particular area of your life?
[See also Librarian, page 237; Books, page 254]

College, university

Higher education may be viewed as learning for its own sake or as a rung on the ladder to greater opportunities.

In your dream: Is your subconscious suggesting that perhaps you need to advance your education in order to take best advantage of your opportunities, at work and in your social life? What were you studying? Is it connected with what you do in waking life or is it something completely different? Are you considering a change of career? Or do you need greater mental stimulation in order to make the most of your abilities? Think about the ramifications before making any major changes!

Museum

Museums hold collections of our joint pasts. Do you find them exciting or boring in waking life?

In your dream: Are you living too much in the past, relying too heavily on 'past glories'? Should you be heeding the lessons of your own personal history in order to avoid making mistakes in the future?

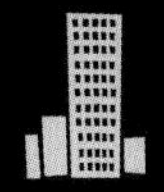

School

How a dream of school is interpreted depends on your own memories. Did you enjoy your schooldays or were you impatient to leave, to get a job and be seen as an adult? Do you now regret not working hard, or did you work too hard and miss out on socializing?

In your dream: Was the dream an actual memory, and if so, what sparked it? Maybe your own children are starting school, or perhaps you met an old schoolfriend recently. Or was the dream more surreal? Were you, for instance, an adult being forced to sit with children at a child-sized desk, being laughed at by the class? Is your subconscious trying to 'teach you a lesson'; are you perhaps trying to 'run before you can walk' when it comes to fulfilling your goals? Perhaps you need to do some research first, find out what is needed and 'go back to school' for a while.

Art gallery

The type of art on display and your familiarity with art and galleries are important in interpreting a dream of them.

In your dream: What kind of art was on display, and did you like it? Did you feel comfortable or out of place? Did this equate with how you would feel in your waking life?

If you were alone, are you feeling isolated in waking life, perhaps viewing the people around you as no more real to you than pictures on a wall or sculptures on plinths?

Your subconscious may be suggesting you take some time to contemplate the works of art – manufactured, natural or human – that surround you.

(See also Artist, page 249)

Restaurant

A restaurant meal is often in celebration of some special occasion and an opportunity to dress up and enjoy fine food.

In your dream: Were you celebrating? Who with? Was the food homely or foreign? Did the meal go smoothly or was it disrupted and if so, by what? Did you enjoy your food, or were you self-conscious, nervous about using the wrong cutlery or spilling your soup? This might imply that you feel 'out of your class', at work or in your social sphere.

Diners at a restaurant are often 'on display', their dress and manners the subject of observation by others. Do you feel yourself constrained to behave courteously in your waking life, to maintain your image?

(See also Food and Drink, page 261; Other People, page 135)

Zoo

Zoos were originally created to study animals and display them to the curious who could never travel to see them in their native environment. Zoos are now more active in preserving animals that are under threat.

In your dream: Did you find the environment constricting or protective? Could the zoo be an image for an aspect of your life? Noisy and hectic, with no escape? Under observation, at work or in your social life? Or are you on the outside of the cage, looking in, observing?

Or is your subconscious suggesting you become involved with conservation work of some kind?

(See also Wild Animals, page 80)

Café

Cafés are more casual than restaurants, good places to meet friends for a snack or informal meal.

In your dream: Was it a cosy **tea house** or a more cosmopolitan pavement **bistro**? If your subconscious supplied the opposite to what you prefer in waking life, are you pretending to be something you aren't?

If the café was dirty or unwelcoming, it may be suggesting you have hygiene or health issues that need to be addressed.

Who did you meet? Or were you alone, watching the world go by? If you lead a hectic and stressful life, dreaming of being in a café may be your mind's way of telling you to slow down a little.

(See also Food and Drink, page 261; Other People, page 135)

Pub

Public houses are generally places to relax and unwind, meet friends and talk – and drink, of course. They can also be threatening places, as too much alcohol can cause aggression and irrationality. Do you visit pubs in your waking life? What do you think of them?

In your dream: Did you enjoy yourself or did you feel frightened or nervous? If the latter, perhaps the dream is a way of your subconscious warning you not to put too much trust in strangers.

(See also Alcohol, page 281)

Hotel

Hotels generally symbolize transience. Hotels are also open to everyone, signifying hospitality.

In your dream: Are you being too hospitable in waking life, perhaps making your time available to anyone who asks, to your own detriment?

If you dream of spending the night at a hotel with a lover, your subconscious may be warning you not to expect the affair to last.

Castle

Castles are designed to keep invaders out and the inhabitants safe.

In your dream: Dreaming of being in a castle suggests firstly, that you see yourself as a strong, defensive individual and secondly, that you feel yourself under siege from outside – especially if you have 'raised the drawbridge' to keep others out.

Palace

Palaces are intimately associated with royalty; they are the homes of kings and queens.

In your dream: Do you see yourself as the **king** or **queen** of your social circle, or is your subconscious telling you that you are worth more than you think?

Or were you there clandestinely, sneaking in to steal something – perhaps the crown itself? Do you desire the power such a position gives you – or the responsibilities? Perhaps you were just visiting, admiring the 'pomp and circumstance' that accompanies royalty but quietly glad you don't have to be on show the whole time.
(See also Crown, page 292)

Tower

Towers are lookouts, designed to give watchers the broadest possible view of the surrounding area, either to prevent attack by hostile forces or to provide a clear view for other purposes (astronomy, for example). Do you see yourself as above others, intellectually or morally? Perhaps you're a protector of some kind, responsible for the safety and well-being of others. A tower, like any other upward-pointing structure such as a spire or chimney, can also symbolize an erection.

In your dream: If the tower is strong and in good repair, it suggests that your faith in yourself to perform your job is sound. If, however, the tower is in disrepair with crumbling steps or stonework, it might be wise to check that you're up to date with all the procedures you need to ensure your own safety as well as other people's.

Stately home

A step down from a palace, stately homes were the dwelling places of the aristocracy, now often open to paying visitors to help with their upkeep.

In your dream: Dreaming of living in a stately home (presuming you don't in waking life) may indicate a wish for a grander, more genteel lifestyle harking back to a less hectic, stressful time.

Lighthouse

Lighthouses save ships from foundering on dangerous rocks and shoals. They are also seen as solitary places to live.

In your dream: Do you see yourself as a '**beacon**' to others – of knowledge, hope or love, perhaps? Are you trying to give someone a warning, maybe about their relationships?

If you were happy as a lighthouse keeper: are you usually a solitary person or was the dream suggesting that a little time alone might be a good thing?

If the dream is recurring perhaps you're suffering from feelings of isolation and loneliness and should seek advice.

Hospital

This may be a common subject if you have recently visited a hospital or are awaiting an operation, or if you are a health professional in your waking life. Otherwise, look for symbolic parallels with an aspect of your life.

In your dream: Were you working there, as a nurse or doctor, for example? Perhaps you see yourself as qualified to intervene in others' lives, emotionally if not physically, perhaps as a surgeon removing the cause of an illness?

If you were a patient, were you well-tended, or was the stay painful and humiliating? The latter may indicate an ailment that should be attended to, no matter how embarrassing.

A hospital may be a subconscious warning to look to your health – perhaps time for a medical check up?

(See also Nurse, Doctor, page 182; Illness, page 154; The Human Body, page 112)

Prison, jail

Incarceration, being behind bars, can indicate guilt or being deprived of your freedom.

In your dream: Were you guilty? Is it a genuine waking-life guilt, or something minor that is nevertheless preying on your mind? Or have others accused you unjustly, and you now feel trapped and exposed to censure? How might you clear your name?

If you were visiting someone else, do you see them as guilty of some act towards you? Do you have them trapped and at your mercy? Where do you plan to go from here?
(See also Police, page 187; Lock, Key, page 300; Punishment, page 156; Vault, page 323)

Factory

We tend to associate factories with unceasing and perhaps noisy machinery, and soulless and robotically repeated tasks. What the factory is producing is significant.

In your dream: Were you working? If so, do you find your current job mind-numbing and soul-destroying, a small cog in a big machine? Or do you admire the efficiency and smooth beauty of the 'machine' and feel proud of your place in it?

If you were feeling lost or threatened, you probably find the relentless nature of technologically based society difficult to cope with. Understanding how it works may be useful in helping you to feel more at home.
(See also Computer, page 232)

High-rise, tower block, skyscraper

Building upwards is an effective way of cramming a lot of people into living or working space without taking up much room on the ground.

In your dream: Living or working in a dream high-rise suggests you feel a little out of touch with the ground. Did you enjoy looking down at the people below or did you feel uneasy at being so high up? Do these metaphors equate with attitudes in your waking life?

Church, mosque, synagogue

These are places of worship specific to single patriarchal deities.

In your dream: If you are a particularly religious person, you might dream of spending time in contemplation if you are troubled by spiritual matters in waking life – if you find yourself being tempted to do something wrong, for example.

Alternatively, if you are there unwillingly, maybe you feel your received religious beliefs are at odds with your deep personal beliefs.

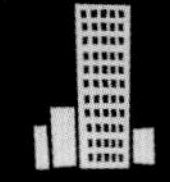

Temple

Temples are usually ancient places of worship, contemplation and meditation, from the great Buddhist sanctuaries to Shinto shrines and Hindu holy places to the classical temples of Greece and Rome. Their significance in dreams depends in part on your own beliefs and how they affect your behaviour.

In your dream: Being in a temple often indicates you are **seeking refuge** from some disturbing matter in waking life. Retreating from it for a while in order to gather your strength is one thing, but living in denial is probably not wise. Does the dream give any indication of how you might be able to deal with the problem?

OUT OF DOORS

Garden, park

Gardens and parks fall half way between man-made structures and the natural world, a kind of 'tamed nature', places to relax and enjoy natural beauty without going all the way.

In your dream: Dreaming of being in a garden suggests that while you appreciate nature, you perhaps are a little mistrustful of its power, its ability to ignore you. In a garden or park, you have control – mostly, anyway!

Cemetery, graveyard

Burial places in dreams are usual symbols of loss and remembrance. A dream involving such a place isn't at all uncommon when there has been a recent death in the family; at other times its meaning depends on the state of the graveyard and how you felt about it.

In your dream: A dark, gloomy place, full of broken or toppled **headstones** might indicate the graveyard of your hopes and ambitions, but equally it can suggest that all the qualities you once disliked about yourself are buried here, especially if it's sunny outside the cemetery.

A well-tended, tranquil cemetery suggests you have adjusted to change and loss in your life, and can look back with nothing more than a little sadness.

If you were visiting the grave of someone you know, were they a friend or someone you disliked? What might the dream be trying to teach you? Not to let the memory of the person die? Or perhaps to forgive them?

(See also Death, page 165; Gravedigger, page 183)

Farm

Farms produce most of the food we need to live. 'Farmhouse' tends to conjure up an image of old-fashioned, easy-going comfort, yet in reality farm life is extremely labour-intensive, hard and the working day protracted.

In your dream: What sort of farm was it and what was your role? Were you providing food for all and sundry or were you 'reaping the rewards' of your past hard work? What does its produce – animal or arable – tell you about yourself and how you view the world? Animals on farms are bred for specific purposes, frequently for slaughter: does that disturb you or is it an accepted part of life? If you're vegetarian and dreamed of working on a farm breeding animals, was it because you wanted to ensure their lives were as happy as they could be or was it a nightmare?
(See also Food and Drink, page 261; Farmer, page 173)

Ranch

The main feature of a dream ranch is probably the landscape – wide open plains or rolling hills with few other people around, where you can enjoy solitude and the natural world while still being at work. Such a dream may be nothing more than a wistful longing to get out of the city, out of your normal working practices, and commune with nature for a while, although the other objects, people and events in the dream will qualify its meaning.

In your dream: What sort of ranch was it – an Australian sheep-ranch with an endless vista of brush, an American cattle ranch, or perhaps a holiday ranch, taking groups of riders **trekking** in the hills?
(See also Horse, page 76)

Stone circle

Whatever their original use, as temples, observatories, calendars or something more esoteric, stone circles have a certain mystery to them. Circular shapes are also considered to be symbolic of the womb.

In your dream: Being within a stone circle may suggest a strong physical or spiritual link to the distant past, possibly a yearning for a supposedly simpler but more meaningful lifestyle, with less responsibility and stress. If the dream is frequent, you might like to consider exploring the significance of stone circles and henges in myth and legend. (See also Circle, page 243)

Pyramid

Pyramids represent humanity reaching for the heavens – for knowledge, wisdom and understanding.

In your dream: Dreaming of climbing up a pyramid symbolizes your striving for self-knowledge, fulfilment; climbing down indicates an awareness that you're backing away from your aspirations. **Being trapped inside a pyramid** suggests that you feel stuck in the past, with all its mistakes and problems, with no way to escape. Remember that there's always a way out, if you hunt for it.

Maze, labyrinth

The idea of the maze is ancient: mazes appear in most cultures. They are sometimes viewed as a metaphor for the journey through life.

In your dream: Being lost in a maze in dreams is more than likely to reflect the fact that you are feeling lost in waking life, unable to find the path, or possibly unable to decide which of several paths is the correct one for you to take. Pay particular attention to the other details of the dream which may offer clues about your options.

Ruins

Ruins in dreams usually represent loss, the wreck of whatever the original structure meant, or a fear of loss.

In your dream: The meaning will depend on what the ruins had once been. A house? A place of worship? Your own home? A dream of a house in ruins may occur, for example, if you're facing financial ruin or a severe medical problem – the 'ruin' of your health. Refer to other appropriate symbols in the book for more information.

Tunnel

Tunnels lead from one place to another, maybe a way of escaping. A tunnel may also symbolize the birth canal.

In your dream: Dreaming of entering or exiting a tunnel may indicate either emerging into the world – 'the light at the end of the tunnel' – perhaps after a long illness, or a desire to return to a pre-birth state with no responsibilities.
(See also Cave, page 31; Door, page 297; Birth, page 151)

Well

Constructed where a natural underground water source comes close to the surface, wells provide the water that makes life possible. Digging wells and making them safe is a communal activity, done for the good of all.

In your dream: Wells can represent creativity and inspiration and the upwelling of emotion. Was the well brimming with satisfying fresh water, freshening and inspiring you to greater efforts; or was the well dry of water and of ideas? If the bucket was full of holes, are you having memory problems?

Did you throw money into the well and make a wish? You may be hoping for the impossible!
(See also Water, page 63)

Bunker, vault

A bunker is, effectively, a man-made cave, but where a cave most often represent the womb, a bunker is somewhere to retreat to when danger threatens: it's the external situation that determines whether a bunker is needed or not.

In your dream: Are you **under threat**, literally or figuratively, in your waking life? Do you feel like going underground and staying there until the 'all clear' sounds? Was anyone else in the dream with you, and if so, is it someone you can trust to help you resolve the problem?

Bridge

In dreams, as in waking life, bridges connect things – the two banks of a river or islands, for example. Their symbolism in dreams is often to connect people or ideas, 'bridging the gulf' of emotional or physical distance or reassuring you that it is possible to reach your goals.

In your dream: Dreaming of a bridge when you find it difficult to achieve a particular ambition is a positive image. What else was in the dream, and how does it help clarify what is needed?

TOOLS AND EQUIPMENT

The term here refers to equipment that makes activities safer or more organized, rather than building or repairing. In dreams, the objects usually represent areas of our lives that need some attention, perhaps to be cleaned up or ordered. More specialized tools are often associated with aspirations, creativity or fears.

Tools in general

Tools apply to the sphere of work: the ability to make and use tools frees humans from a lot of hard physical labour, giving us more time to spend on leisure activities. The use of tools in dreams can be very significant.

In your dream: Consider the circumstances. If, for example, you spend most of your time in a sedentary occupation but dreamed of digging in a field or garden, your subconscious may very well be telling you to get out and be more active before your body suffers. However, if you were dressed in a suit and smart shoes, or digging in an inappropriate place – the middle of the office, perhaps – it may suggest that you are literally using 'the wrong tools for the job' and need to reappraise your work practices and ethics!

Spade, shovel

The basic digging tool, used by gardeners, farmers, labourers and gravediggers. Why you were digging will shed light on the meaning of the activity.

In your dream: If you were **digging a garden** to grow your own vegetables or flowers, do you feel the need to be more self-reliant or do you need more beauty in your life?

Were you perhaps **digging for treasure**, maybe the treasures to be found in your own mind if you can just uncover them?

If you were **digging a grave**, was it for yourself? Are you 'digging your own grave' through your actions in waking life – at work or in your relationships with other people? If you were digging a grave for someone else, are you symbolically burying a friendship that has ended? Alternatively, is it for someone you wish were dead (at least to you)? Is it a relationship that can be salvaged or has it gone too far?

Was the soil solid and hard to shift, or so sandy it filled the hole as soon as you'd made it? The former may suggest that you're finding it very hard to make progress, the latter that it seems to be easy but you are in fact going nowhere.

Saw

Similar to shears but used for larger plants, for cutting down trees and shaping wood.

In your dream: Using a saw may indicate a need to dispose of 'deadweight' – people who are holding you back.

Shears, secateurs

These are tools for pruning, cutting back dead or diseased growth, or deadheading old flowers.

In your dream: The symbolism is fairly straightforward: if you're using them in a dream, it most likely represents your need to carry out **pruning** in your work or the way you perform it, discarding old, outworn practices in favour of newer, more efficient ones. Of course, you need to be careful when doing so, to avoid cutting too far and damaging healthy growth as well!

Fork

The garden or farm fork is used for turning soil to prepare it for planting, rather than digging, or for moving material such as hay or straw. It's a lighter tool than a spade, both in physical weight and in its use.

In your dream: A fork it may represent your wish to 'fork over' your work, pulling out any obstacles – 'weeds' and 'stones' – that prevent the smooth flow of projects.

Rake, hoe

Used to break up the soil, rakes and hoes make it easier to remove weeds and keep the plants healthy.

In your dream: A rake or hoe is likely to have the metaphorical meaning. Might it mean 'raking in the cash' – here applied to gains earned through your own efforts, rather than through gambling – or 'a hard row to hoe', suggesting that the particular project you are engaged in is going to be difficult to bring to fruition. Is there a way to improve matters?

Farm machinery

Most farm machinery performs the same functions as the tools above, but on a much larger, heavier scale.

In your dream: Dreaming of operating equipment such as a **plough**, **combine harvester** or **chainsaw** suggests that you know your projects will need a major input of work and resources to bring them to completion. If you were comfortable operating the machinery, you're probably both competent and confident enough to manage. However, if you were having problems, it might be wise to rethink your methods and ask for help.

Hammer

From hammering in nails to manipulating a chisel, the hammer is a very basic but versatile tool. Its significance in a dream depends in part on what you were doing with it, but generally speaking a hammer indicates a need to act forcefully to solve problems.

In your dream: Were you wielding a hammer in order to 'hammer out' difficulties or 'hammer into shape' projects that seem ill-defined and lacking in focus and direction? (See also Blacksmith, page 189)

Chisel

The stoneworker's and sculptor's tool.

In your dream: A chisel usually represents a need to 'chisel away' at a project, trimming away erroneous material until the true shape comes into view.

Spirit level, plumb line

Both are used to ensure flat level surfaces and correct angles in building.

In your dream: These useful tools may act as a subconscious nudge to make sure the career you're building for yourself is stable and 'on the level'.

Screwdriver

The one tool no modern home should lack. From fixing shelves to walls to changing fuses in plugs, without a screwdriver life becomes surprisingly difficult. It also has fairly obvious sexual connotations.

In your dream: Using a screwdriver competently in a dream suggests that you feel capable of dealing with the day-to-day problems of waking life – or in your sex life, if the screwdriver is a sexual symbol in your dream. Being unable to find the tool or not able to use it properly, may indicate difficulties in your work or sex life.

Its presence may also have the meaning of saying 'Screw you' to another person in the dream!

Scales

The meaning of scales as the focus of a dream depends on what was being weighed. Scales also stand for justice. Justice is represented by a blindfolded figure holding a pair of scales, symbolizing that justice is impartial. This image may appear in dreams if you feel you've suffered injustice or are awaiting the outcome of legal action.

In your dream: If you were weighing yourself, are you concerned about your weight? It might be wise to reconsider your diet. Weighing food also suggests a concern with diet, but with the value of the food you eat, a well-balanced diet – less junk food and more fresh fruit and vegetables, perhaps?

Alternatively, is your subconscious warning you that something in your life is out of balance? Or perhaps you are being 'weighed in the balance and found wanting' – not capable of fulfilling your responsibilities?

Drill

Drills are used for making holes so that different materials may be attached to each other. The shape and action of a drill also make it another contender for a sexual symbol, but the force behind the tool can suggest its use may be dangerous if not under tight control.

In your dream: Using a drill may suggest you feel yourself responsible for bringing together the disparate elements of a project and ensuring they all work together correctly. Alternatively, you might simply be reminding yourself to tackle that repair job you've been putting off!

In a sexual context, dreaming of a drill puncturing the wrong material or causing damage by drilling too hard and fast may be a warning to practise safe sex.

Nails, screws

These metal fixings may be small and inconspicuous, but without them things fall apart. In dreams they often symbolize the people who work behind the scenes, the 'invisibles' who keep everything moving smoothly.

In your waking life: Does something need to be repaired in your working life? Is a project falling apart and in need of shoring up?

(See also Repairman, page 172)

HOUSEHOLD EQUIPMENT AND FURNITURE

Paint and paintbrushes

Whether employed to create a work of art, decorate a building, brighten a dull space or mute a light one, or to cover up blemishes, paint covers the initial façade to produce a specific effect. Painting can disguise or hide original surfaces.

In your dream: Were you painting a large blank space? At work or at home? This could simply suggest that you need a 'change of scenery' in your daily life, but nothing as dramatic or traumatic as moving house or job.

If faced with a blank canvas, brushes and an **artist's palette**, your subconscious may be suggesting that you need an outlet for your **creativity**. Were you in a class of art students or alone? Did you paint or did the canvas remain blank? Are you being given the opportunity to express yourself in waking life, at work or in your leisure time, to do something that will 'make your mark' on your career or your life?

Wallpaper

Wallpaper can be very tricky to use. In dreams it's often a visual symbol of 'papering over the cracks' in a relationship, a job or other element of life.

In your dream: Even if you were wallpapering successfully, it might be worth considering what you're trying to hide, and whether it's ultimately worth the effort.

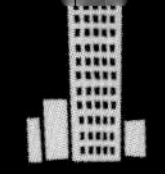

Batteries

An essential of our time, batteries can be used to power equipment from a torch to a car.

In your dream: Dreaming of running out of batteries, especially in a place where so many things require them, suggests you feel ill-equipped to deal with the requirements of the job at hand.
(See also Electrician, page 171)

Torch, lamp

These objects 'shed light' on the matter at hand, both in waking life and in dreams.

In your dream: What was the light's beam revealing? Flaws and shortcomings you might be trying to hide? Or skills and talents you are afraid to reveal, in case others think them of no significance?

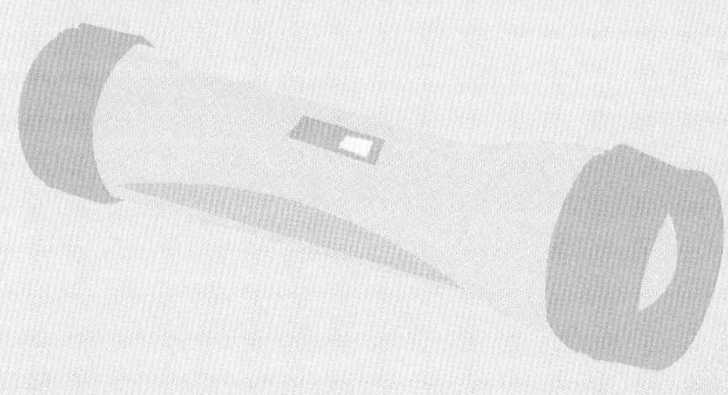

Sieve, filter

These tools sift good from bad: wheat from chaff, gold from sand, hiss from pure sound. A sieve is hand-held, personally controlled, while filter is usually more remote: an email filter on a computer, for example, a water or coffee filter, or the sound filters on a music player.

In your dream: A sieve suggests you may need to 'sieve through' something in your waking life, to sort out the important from the trivial – whether people, material possessions, memories or work. Were you perhaps panning for 'gold', the things that are of real value to you?

Any kind of filter suggests you may be unconsciously filtering what reaches you. Are you filtering out too much, perhaps, disregarding important information in the process?

Cushion, pillow

Cushions represent comfort, a support while you are relaxing. An uncomfortable pillow will lead to restless sleep and an aching neck. Pillows also suggest a more intimate theme, as your bed is an intimate place.

In your dream: Were you at ease on the cushions or unable to find a comfortable position? Do you feel that taking time off for yourself is well-deserved or somehow naughty, a guilty pleasure? Consider how to consciously make yourself relax, in order to stave off stress.

If pillows featured, were you alone or enjoying a little 'pillow talk' with a bed-mate? Was the dream suggesting you spend more time sleeping or talking to your lover?

Knife

As with most tools, knives can be used for good or harm: a knife and fork makes for easier, more polite table manners, while a switchblade can be terrifying, even deadly.

In your dream: Were you being threatened or threatening someone else with a knife? This may not necessarily mean someone is physically a threat in your waking life – it may be that someone's 'cutting wit' or sarcastic attitude is making life uncomfortable or that a friend is trying to 'cut you out of their life'.

Using a knife creatively, to shape wood for a sculpture, or pastry for cooking, indicates a possibly hidden artistic bent.

Curtains, blinds

Window dressings are decorative but from a dream perspective, it is the privacy they afford that is their main significance.

In your dream: Were the curtains shutting out light or stopping people staring in? Are you hiding, not wanting people to see what you are doing or how you live? Have you screened off one part of your life, not wanting to acknowledge its existence? Filmy net curtains can allow you to look out, but not in. Who or what were you watching from inside and why?

Alternatively, is your subconscious saying it's 'curtains' for something or someone?

If you dreamed of blinds, are you 'blinding' yourself to something or someone?

Needle

In most cases a needle is a positive image in a dream. Needles are used either to sew things together, as in making clothes or stitching a wound, or as a hypodermic, injecting whatever is needed to assist healing.

In your dream: Depending on the circumstances surrounding the image, your subconscious might be suggesting that it's time to prepare for a forthcoming event – by getting holiday injections or acquiring new clothes, for example – or by making repairs to prevent problems in the future.

Dreaming of injecting drugs, however, may be a warning that you are trying to escape into fantasy to avoid the problems in your waking life.

Scissors

Scissors are generally a positive image in dreams; they are useful, creative implements. However, since a mis-cut – malicious or accidental – can ruin an otherwise excellent haircut or fabric, wielders of a pair of scissors also possess a degree of power over the material they're cutting.

In your dream: Were you using the scissors yourself? With flair and expertise, or gingerly and awkwardly? If the latter, do you feel confident of your ability to 'make the cut' in your professional life or do you need to gain more confidence and experience?

(See also Hairdresser, page 178)

Scalpel

These extremely sharp precision instruments are primarily used by surgeons. Regardless of how necessary its use might be – in a life-saving operation, for example – the scalpel is never a friendly image, as much because it usually involves entrusting your body to another as because of its inherent danger.

In your dream: Was the scalpel being used on yourself: was it to heal or harm? Is someone harming you by 'cutting off' something important to you: a relationship or your possibilities of promotion, perhaps?

Were you wielding the scalpel? Perhaps to cut away something holding you back or something dead? Were you successful or was it a messy, painful procedure? The former suggests that you are confident in your ability to deal with the problem: the latter that you're afraid of making a disaster of the matter.

If you were using it to cut yourself, it might be wise to see a healthcare expert.

Pin

Pins are temporary articles, used to hold things together until they can be properly secured.

In your dream: Were there a lot of pins in the dream? Were they stabbing you? Such a dream, especially if recurrent, may suggest personal insecurity, or that the 'fabric' of your life is held together in the flimsiest way and needs to be reappraised.

Dreaming of **picking up pins** suggests a thrifty nature – unless you were dropping them, in which case the dream may be suggesting you learn to be thrifty!

Telephone

The main symbol of mechanical communication, in waking life as in dreams.

In your dream: Does the image of the phone make you feel guilty or anxious? Are you waiting for someone to get in touch with you? Is there someone you've been meaning to call but haven't found the time? Are you putting off dealing with an unpleasant or distasteful task? If so, it may be better to make the call and deal with the problem: the longer you leave it, the more difficult it will become.

Sound system

Record player, radio, stereo, walkman, MP3 player: whichever you choose in a dream will indicate your familiarity with the technology and how comfortable you feel with it as a whole.

In your dream: An antique gramophone or old record player suggests an appreciation of history and the simplicity and solidity of the old media; enjoying the use of the latest music players indicates feeling at ease with modern technology.

A music system of any kind suggests that music is important in your life, but even more that having control is significant to you, even if it's only to turn a dial to another frequency.

CD, DVD

Both disks represent a way to save and protect sound and images for later playback. In dreams they symbolize both memory and entertainment.

In your dream: What sort of disk did the dream involve – a computer disk for storing information, a music disk to play while working or driving, or a film to watch while relaxing with friends? The first may indicate a need to organize your life. A music or video disk suggests the importance of audio or visual stimulation in your life. Were you buying them yourself, suggesting a wish for something new in life, or sorting through a collection to find a particular memory or favourite song, indicating a nostalgic spell?

HOUSEHOLD IMPLEMENTS

Brush, broom

Brooms are used to clean the floor, but they move dirt around rather than sucking it away.

In your dream: Are you 'sweeping things under the carpet'? Your subconscious may be warning you that it would be better to bring them out into the open and deal with them.

Iron

Ironing flattens out unattractive creases and makes the crumpled smooth and smart.

In your dream: Do you perhaps need to 'iron out the creases' or 'wrinkles' in your life? If you've been 'wearing a disguise', is your subconscious suggesting that it's rumpled and allowing people to see behind it? Or is it time to 'straighten out' your relationships with others?
(See also Clothes, page 283)

Vacuum cleaner

A vacuum cleaner removes dirt from the floor, often dirt that people have walked in from the outside.

In your dream: Vacuuming the floor suggests you feel that you or others have soiled the underpinning of your life, making it less easy to keep your feet or walk comfortably in your home. By cleaning up you are taking steps to restore things to their original ordered state.

Vacuuming in another person's home may indicate you suspect things aren't as wholesome in their life as appears.

Washing machine

While a bath cleans the person, a washing machine cleans the things they wear. In dreams, these may include ideas, beliefs, opinions, politics, the way we wish to be perceived

In your dream: To have a washing machine as the focus of a dream suggests an awareness that one or more elements in your life may need a thorough 'washing', to clean it of clinging dirt and stains.

Bucket

Buckets are useful, everyday items, generally holding water or waste material.

In your dream: If the bucket was full of waste, it may suggest your subconscious is advising you to get rid of any waste in your life – a long-held, festering grudge, perhaps. (See also Water, page 63; Well, page 322)

Toys

As children, toys helped us learn a little about the world, or kept us entertained. As adults we may look back on them with nostalgia or replace them with adult versions.

In your dream: As an adult, a dream of children's toys, especially soft toys, can indicate a longing either for a child, or a return to a child-like state. Educational toys suggest a wish to shape and reform your world, make it more to your liking. A dream of 'executive toys' such as Newton's Cradle or decision-making devices indicate a wish to have the stress of work relieved, while adult, sexual toys suggest you yearn for some spice in your sex life!

Rope, cord

Ropes and cords have many uses and are associated with feelings of security in a number of forms.

In your dream: Was the rope helping you to climb up or abseil down? Did your life depend on it remaining securely fastened? Was it wrapping a parcel, stopping you from seeing what was inside, or perhaps holding back an animal that would otherwise attack you? If so, it might be that you are feeling insecure at the moment, maybe 'dangling by a thread'. If the rope was in a tug-of-war, do you feel yourself being pulled in two directions? You may need to make a decision soon.

If you dreamed of cord, does it represent tying something, a **pull-cord** to attract attention, or an **umbilical cord**? If the latter, are you too dependent on someone close, whether willingly or not?

Fan

There is a wide variety of fans, all with their own slightly different meanings.

In your dream: Fans from around the world suggest different things. Oriental fans suggest simple sophistication and stillness. A Spanish lace fan indicates a passionate nature. An elaborate English fan suggests flirtation and playfulness.

A hand-held electric fan symbolizes practicality: you're happy to have technology take care of the tedious things present in your life.

A ceiling fan can suggest a leisurely approach to life, whereas a free-standing electric fan can indicate a need for a breath of fresh air in your life.

A dream of problems with **air-conditioning** suggests that things are 'heating up' somehow in your life, and not in a beneficial way.

Glue

Glue sticks two things together, seals openings and repairs breaks.

In your dream: Were you 'sticking to someone like glue'? Or trying to mend something important that was broken, such as a heart or a gift? How did you feel?

Was the glue preventing you from doing something? A not unusual dream is to find your lips glued together, usually when you need to warn about a pending disaster. Or perhaps your glued fingers were preventing you handling or touching anything. If the pages of a book were glued together, are you perhaps looking for advice where none is forthcoming? If you were sticking stamps on envelopes, do you need to contact someone?

Diary, journal

A diary or journal is a way of recording your life, what you do and feel as you grow. It can also act as a useful record for future generations, or it can help you to sort through your feelings by the simple act of writing them down.

In your dream: A lockable diary suggests you have secrets too exciting not to record, but are afraid of others knowing them. Someone reading your private diary aloud indicates you know the person isn't to be trusted.

Bottle

The style and contents of bottles can vary the interpretation.

In your dream: An elegant bottle of expensive perfume suggests a need for elegance in your life, while a half-full milk bottle indicates a need to pay more attention to the basics of life!

An empty bottle indicates disappointment, the draining away of your hopes and wishes. A bottle that you can't open suggests a subconscious awareness that you're unprepared for the opportunities presented to you.

Table

Tables can be associated with meals or family get-togethers, and also as a focus for negotiations or decision-making.

In your waking life: Are you 'putting all your cards on the table', being completely open and honest about work or relationship affairs? Or are you hiding under it, afraid or unwilling to face the truth?

Cooker, oven

Ovens are a source of sustenance and warmth. They symbolize nurturing and even new life – 'a bun in the oven'.

In your dream: Are you expecting a child or perhaps want one? Or is the oven cold and unused? Perhaps you are not giving your loved ones the care and attention they need or that you need? If you feel chained to it, are family or friends expecting you to slave over them too much?

Refrigerator

These are designed to keep things cold, and suggest ice in a controlled or domestic setting rather than the untamed wild.

In your dream: Is your subconscious suggesting you 'stay cool' in an inflammable situation? Do you need to 'put something on ice' – a grudge or personal feelings, for example?
(See also Icescape, page 31)

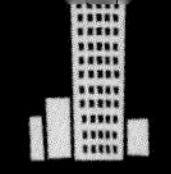

Chair

Chairs generally relate to your current state of mind.

In your dream: Were you relaxed in an easy chair, or 'on the edge of your seat' with nerves, fear or apprehension? Were you **'in the chair'**, facing torture or death and if so, what do you feel you did that was so dreadful you deserve such a fate? A **rocking chair** may indicate that you feel that you're getting old, or simply find the action soothing?

Were you the only person standing in a room full of seated people? If so, do you feel exposed, as though there's a spotlight shining down on you? Are the people around you expecting too much of you?

Bath

The two main aspects of a bath, in dreams as in waking life, are as a place to get clean and an enjoyable way to wind down and release muscle tension.

In your dream: Were you enjoying a relaxing soak, perhaps with a favourite book and glass of wine, or were you cleaning yourself? Do you feel the need to scrub yourself clean of something you've done that you regret – yet which will still taint you, as symbolized by the bathwater in which you sit, rather than being swept away down the plughole as would be the case when washing under a shower?
(See also Waterfall, page 28)

Bed

The bed is both a place to sleep and a place to have sex: consider which of the two the bed in the dream meant to you.

In your dream: It may simply be that your subconscious is urging you to rest. If you saw the bed as a place of intimacy, did you enjoy it or feel guilty? What is your attitude towards sex in your waking life? Is your subconscious warning you to be a little more discerning in your choice of partner or activity, or advising you to enjoy yourself more?

Mirror

Mirrors let us see our own reflection, allow us to see behind us without turning around, and brighten dark spaces by reflecting light. They've been associated with magic for millennia, and even today hold a fascination for the imaginative mind.

In your dream: What was the mirror's purpose in the dream? To distort images? To check your appearance – and if so, did it show you as you are or as you wish to be? Can you take any steps to achieve that form? Did you, like Lewis Carroll's Alice, step through the looking glass into a new world? Or did it show you shapes behind you, perhaps things you've been trying to deny or ignore?

Crib, child-carrier

If you are responsible for a child, dreaming of a crib or baby-carrier, whether a sling or a pram or buggy, is likely to simply be a reflection of your waking life. If you are not and are not expecting a child, the dream suggests you see someone in your life – an elderly parent, lover or partner – as a child, needing the same attention as a baby.

In your dream: Were you resentful or happy to have the situation continue?

If the crib or carrier was faulty, squeaking or too big and heavy to handle easily, are you having problems in your dealings with those who depend on you? Do you need a break from the responsibility?

Strong box, safe, vault

All three are methods of keeping valuables safe, helping to prevent the theft of money or certificates, jewellery, antiques or works of art. While they may help give you peace of mind, they have the disadvantage of not allowing you to enjoy the very things you are locking away.

In your dream: What was in the safe? Had someone persuaded you to store something precious there against your inner wishes? Or do you wish you had a safe to keep your valuables out of harm's way?

A dream of **being locked in a vault** suggests you feel stifled, shut away to keep you safe by someone who loves you but is afraid to give you any freedom.

12 RITUAL, CEREMONY AND CELEBRATION

The human race has observed rituals for millennia. Rites of passage were probably the earliest. Later came ceremonies to mark notable times of the year, and rituals to honour deities developed, which are still practised today. A few of the most widespread rituals are included here, along with common religious symbols drawn from several faiths. The list is in no way exhaustive, but may help to illuminate otherwise puzzling dreams.

Most people have been subjected to religious imagery during their lives, so it's not surprising that such images crop up in dreams from time to time, whether or not you are a believer – most also have a non-religious significance.

Bell, whistle

Bells and whistles can act as alarms or they can summon us or they can be an indicator of time. For many, school bells or playing field whistles were a familiar measure of time in childhood.

In your dream: If you dreamed of a **bell**, what form did it take? A church bell calling people to pray? If so, your subconscious may be advising you to give some consideration to your emotional and spiritual side. An alarm bell warning of forthcoming danger – a storm or a fire, perhaps – may be warning you of problems ahead. A school bell suggests you may need to put in some study, while an alarm clock's bell suggests you may need to 'wake up' to what's happening around you.
(See also Being Early/Late, page 248)

Were you 'blowing the whistle' on someone or something? Did you miss the starting **whistle** or gun and were left behind? Or was it a referee's whistle, warning you to moderate your behaviour?

Stigmata

Stigmata is the term for what appear to be bleeding holes in the hands and feet of an individual, symbolic of the nail wounds in the hands and feet of the crucified Jesus.

In your dream: The stigmata may indicate suffering or an identification with the deity.
(See also Hands page 118; Feet page 123)

Crucifix

Crucifixion was a drawn-out, brutal method of torture and execution, and a cross with the figure of Jesus on it, often worn as jewellery, symbolizes sacrifice and redemption.

In your dream: To believers, a crucifix in a dream suggests the dreamer may be worrying about their 'sins' or if the feeling associated with the image is hopeful or happy, the love of their deity. Alternatively, do you feel as if you are being 'crucified', made the scapegoat for everything that goes wrong at work or in the family?

The less extreme version, a **cross** shape with no figure, often symbolizes a crossroads in your life, a time to choose which path you wish to take.

[See also Places, Crossroads, page 21]

Priest

Here, the term is used to include vicar, pope, guru, missionary or any other person with a responsibility for the spiritual well-being of others and advancement of those who have placed themselves in his/her care. It's an occupation that can, unfortunately, be open to a lot of abuse.

In your dream: If you dreamed of being a priest or priestess do you hold a position in waking life where you are privy to a lot of confidential information? Do people trust you with their secrets? Are you tempted to break that confidence? Do you find it a burden or are you happy to deal with it? Who do you trust to keep your own secrets – and are they doing so?

Angels

Angels are messengers in a number of religions.

In your dream: In dreams they may represent messengers from your subconscious to yourself, in a form that you may find easier to trust if you aren't used to relying on your own instincts. It's important to watch what they do and listen to anything they say.

Font

A font becomes the focus of attention in a church when a new Christian is brought for baptism, usually as a baby.

In your dream: A font can symbolize acceptance into a religious faith, cleansing of the soul if you are a believer, the mind and psyche if you aren't or the spiritual duties of parenthood.

Communion bread and wine

The bread and wine of the Christian Communion, or Mass, represent the body and blood of Jesus, partaken in remembrance of his sacrifice 'to save the world from sin'.

In your dream: Dreaming of being at a Communion service may indicate a wish to join the community or an uneasiness with religious ritual if you felt out of place.

Symbolic fish

Fish have several symbolic religious meanings. The simple fish symbol of two curved lines touching at one end and intersecting at the other has been adopted as a Christian symbol, but is actually much older, and once represented the womb of the mother goddess.

In your dream: Traditionally used as a signal of recognition between Christians in times of persecution, for a believer the appearance of a fish may indicate a feeling of being under threat because of your beliefs. **Two golden fish** facing each other symbolize, happiness, unity, abundance and fertility.

Menorah

The Judaic seven-branched candelabrum is a symbol of teaching by example not by force, and of the eternal light of the faith.

In your dream: It may suggest you are searching for such an example to follow or a reminder of the light of faith.

Burning bush, pillar of fire

In the Jewish religion, these are symbols of the deity's presence, miraculous power and guidance.

In your dream: A burning bush or pillar may suggest a warning not to be reckless or to trust your own 'inner light'.

Hamesh (hamsa) hand

Not exclusively a Jewish symbol but popular in the faith, the hand with an eye in the middle of the palm, worn as an amulet, has been a talisman for luck and to avert hostile psychic influence for millennia.

In your dream: If it appears in a dream, your subconscious may be warning you to take precautions: someone wishes you harm.

Star and crescent

The star and crescent only became a symbol of Islam in the 15th century (prior to that it was a combination of the crescent of Diana and the star of the Virgin Mary).

In your dream: To non-Muslims, its appearance in dreams can suggest a fear of the unknown or more positively, dedication to one's own ideals.

Holy book

The appearance of any holy book – such as the Bible, Torah or Qur'an – in a dream suggests knowledge.

In your dream: Was the book open or closed? Are you open to the knowledge and wisdom to be gained from an open mind in concert with a studious and reverent attitude or is your mind closed?

Dharma wheel

The Buddhist eight-spoked 'wheel of law' represents the eight-fold path to enlightenment, the cycle of birth-death-rebirth and the overcoming of obstacles.

In your dream: The meaning of the Dharma wheel depends on the personal beliefs of the dreamer and the circumstances in the dream. Spinning, the wheel can symbolize cycles; moving, it generally represents progress.

Magen David (Shield or Star of David)

A more recent Jewish image, the Star of David is created from two interlocking triangles, one pointing up, the other pointing down, symbolizing unity of mind and spirit. **(See Triangle, page 244).**

In your dream: The significance will depend on your personal feelings and other symbols in the dream. The Star of David may suggest exile or hope and promise or the horrors of the Holocaust and by extension, crimes of hatred and intolerance.

Umbrella

In Buddhism the white umbrella is a symbol of both royalty and protection.

In your dream: This umbrella represents protection from the elements, but in the sense of the emotions of others, rather than from rain.

Mandala

A mandala is a circle with designs inside it. It's an old design and has been used around the world by many different cultures. It may appear on a wall or woven into a carpet or rug, or it may assume a more esoteric form, floating in mid-air, or even stretching outwards with you as its centre. A circular ornamental maze, its walls not high enough to be useful as a proper maze, may be a mandala.

It symbolizes many different things: the universe, the human psyche, the journey from life to death and possible rebirth, the fully integrated and balanced individual, a focus for meditation or a representation of the mysteries of life.

In your dream: Its meaning should be instinctively recognized; if not, it may simply be a symbol that there is far more for you to learn about yourself and the world in which you live.

Colours and the images within the mandala are important. Make a note of them and consider what they mean to you. (See also Colours, page 255; Shapes, page 243)

Lotus

The lotus encompasses three elements: its roots are buried in mud, its stalk rises through water and the flower blooms in the air.

In your dream: In dreams, as in waking life, this beautiful flower represents enlightenment, personal growth and understanding.

Ankh

The ankh is the ancient Egyptian symbol for Life.

In your dream: It may suggest new life or a symbolic 'rebirth' of the dreamer into a different faith, philosophy or phase of life.

Eye of Horus

The ancient Egyptian symbol is worn in the form of jewellery as a protective amulet.

In your dream: Seeing this image in a dream may indicate either that someone is looking after you, even if you haven't consciously realized it, or if you are wearing it, that you need to take steps to protect yourself, especially your health.

Cauldron

To Wiccans, the cauldron symbolizes birth and abundance.

In your dream: A cauldron may suggest pregnancy, wealth or generous hospitality. It's always a positive image.

Wand, staff

The Wiccan wand or staff symbolizes willpower and the directing of that willpower into making things happen (which is the origin of the notion of the magic wand).

In your dream: As in waking life, the wand represents an implement to direct your personal energy into your activities.

Pentagram

The five-pointed star. Worn with one point upwards and two down, it symbolizes perfected humanity: with two up and one down it has come to represent Satanic worship, which is an offshoot of Christianity (there is no 'devil' in Wicca, only negative impulses that come from within the individual and which the individual is responsible for overcoming).

In your dream: A pentagram can symbolize striving for self-understanding or an interest in the occult.

Party

Parties are typically brief respites from the concerns of daily life, an opportunity to celebrate something – an anniversary, a promotion, a move or simply being alive.

In your dream: A party dream may simply anticipate a real event, either looked forward to or dreaded depending on whether you like parties or are happy or unhappy about the event. Dreaming that you're the recipient of a surprise party suggests you feel unappreciated or if you're unhappy about the occasion, under too much scrutiny. If you dream of throwing the party yourself, it suggests you need to be a little more organized!

Balloon

Quite why balloons are considered appropriate for parties is debatable, but they are nevertheless an enduring fashion.

In your dream: Were the balloons used for a specific celebration – heart-shaped Valentine's day balloons, for example? Were they being used to make animals or other shapes? Does this suggest a wish to shape the insubstantial and fragile to your will?

Fireworks

Fireworks originated in China around two thousand years ago, and have been used in celebrations ever since. They arrived in Europe in the 13th century and became popular in England during the reign of Elizabeth I in the 16th century. They were originally used to scare off evil spirits; these days they light up the sky to see in the New Year or to commemorate notable dates

In your dream: Dream fireworks may simply indicate a celebration, but they can also indicate a certain tension: they're beautiful, but can be dangerous. 'Fireworks' has come to mean an upset, a volatile outburst, often at work. Is this the meaning in your dream? Are you anticipating an unpleasant interview?

Birthday

Everyone has a birthday. It marks the transition between the safe, enclosed life in the womb and the exciting, dangerous life in the outside world, and is the first major rite of passage in our lives. Many people look forward to the celebration of their birthdays for the presents and parties.

In your dream: Happy anticipation in the dream suggests a youthful, child-like temperament that takes pleasure in life; dreading it suggests a fear that you have accomplished nothing in the past year – or in your life - and perhaps ought to remedy the situation before any more time is wasted.

Wedding

The entering of two people into a (hopefully) life-long union is a major rite of passage, indicative of leaving behind a life of independence and self-centredness and entering into a contract involving interdependence, responsibility and cooperation. The celebration surrounding the undertaking is enjoyable but secondary.

In your dream: What a wedding dream symbolizes depends on your role within it. Getting married and feeling happy about it suggests you feel competent to deal with life-changing events; being unhappy or feeling you are being forced into the union indicates reluctance or fear of facing life's responsibilities – or of growing up or losing your freedom. Happy dreams of others getting married indicate contentment with your own status; unhappy dreams suggest you feel you may be being left behind as others move on, in itself indicative of feeling you need to conform whether you wish to or not.

Christmas, Yule, winter solstice

The winter solstice is the longest night of the year and the midwinter celebration, whether Yule, Kwanzaa, Christmas, Hanukah or any other form of celebration, are a highlight of the year.

In your dream: Dreaming of all the trappings of the festivity, the sense of community and excitement it fosters suggests a nostalgic longing for security and stability.

Easter

Originally a spring rebirth festival, Easter was appropriated by the Christians to mark the resurrection of Jesus.

In your dream: Accompanied by images of chicks and rabbits, a dream of Easter may be symbolic of new life and fertility, and spring flowers appearing from ground that may still have a covering of snow. The dream represents hope, optimism and creativity.

Hallowe'en, Samhain

Now overly commercialized as a festival for children, Samhain was originally a time when the boundaries between the world of the living and the world of the dead grew thin, and people could pass between the two.

In your dream: Dreaming of a Hallowe'en celebration may indicate a wish to communicate with someone who has died or to be more receptive to the dark side of yourself. (See also The Supernatural, page 368 and The Shadow, page 148)

Baptism, confirmation, bar/bat mitzvah

These are ceremonies to welcome an individual into a religious community, and mark an important transition in spiritual life.

In your dream: Dreaming of baptism suggests a desire to be cleansed and make a new start in your waking life, while the other ceremonies may indicate a wish for acceptance into the community and the status of an adult, with all its privileges and responsibilities.

Funeral, wake

Funerals are sad affairs, as we say goodbye to someone we have known in life. In a dream, this image can be symbolic of any sort of loss or the end of something.

In your dream: If you haven't had a bereavement recently, dreaming of a funeral usually suggests the need to end something in your waking life – a relationship, perhaps? (See also Mortician, page 183)

13 THE SUPERNATURAL

Things and beings out of the ordinary are found in all cultures across the world and are firmly established in the public consciousness. They often represent the things we wish could exist, or frighten us because they symbolize the darker side of ourselves. Whether we believe in the supernatural or not, it fulfils a need in all of us for something in life to remain mysterious, unknowable – in our dreams, if not in our lives.

Unicorn

One of the best loved of all mythical creatures, the unicorn has come to represent a variety of sometimes conflicting qualities – purity, perfection, mystery, gentleness, strength, divinity, wisdom, good fortune or strict judgement. Above these, though, it symbolizes freedom. Traditionally very hard to capture and ferocious in its efforts to evade or escape hunters, the creature could only be tamed by someone as pure as itself.

The usual reason for wanting to capture a unicorn was the magical properties of its horn – the source of its power.

In your dream: Consider the setting, any other people in the dream, what the unicorn was doing. If you were alone, did the unicorn represent an aspect of yourself – your soul or psyche, for example? Was it trying to teach or show you something or guide you? If you were in a group, were you hunting the unicorn or did the creature symbolize you? Are others trying to 'hunt' you down to take away your freedom? If it was trapped and you freed it, what were you were setting free – your inspiration or creativity, perhaps?

Dragon

Like unicorns, dragons are a very ancient and widespread symbol. Although occasionally benevolent they are usually considered to be malevolent, if not actually evil.

In your dream: If the dragon was causing devastation, is someone making your waking life a misery? If it was guarding a hoard of treasure, are you refusing to share your talents with those around you – perhaps because you see them as unworthy? Or was it benign, protecting you from your enemies?

Centaur

The centaurs were wild and lustful and tended towards drunken violence. Chiron, however, is the centaur everyone remembers; he was the healer and astrologer – wise, noble, compassionate and a trusted tutor to young heroes. Chiron symbolizes strength and intelligence in equilibrium and humanity in control of its animal nature, rising above the urges of the body, while any other centaur represents the victory of physical lust over intellect and sensitivity.

In your dream: What was the centaur doing? How was it behaving? What were your feelings towards it? To dream of riding a centaur implies either self-confidence in your own ability to control yourself and those around you, or the thrill of being under the control of someone or something powerful and with a touch of the primitive, yet restrained.

Satyr

The half-man, half-goat creature of Greek myth, satyrs were lustful beings who inhabited woods and mountains, and enjoyed drinking and merry-making.

In your dream: The satyr may represent an older man who is making unwelcome sexual advances.

Lamia, siren, harpy

The lamia was half-snake, half-woman, and ensnared men and crushed them to death. The sirens and harpies were half-bird, half-women, creatures whose beautiful singing lured men to their death, often on submerged rocks in the sea.

In your dream: These alluring but dangerous creatures usually represent a threatening person, often a woman who is using physical charms or sex to hurt or destroy the dreamer.

Vampire

Creatures that suck the blood of the living to hold onto life vary in depiction from the brutal, terrifying killer to the debonair, erotic lover.

In your dream: A vampire dream can involve both predation and sacrifice. What form did the vampire take? Were you an unwilling victim or perhaps a vampire yourself, sucking others dry? Or did you willingly give your 'life-blood' to help another to survive, and if so, why? Is the vampire someone you know, a dependant perhaps? Or does the notion of giving something so intimate and vital make you feel closer to a loved one?

Incubus, succubus

Originally devised as an explanation for erotic dreams, these are 'demons', male and female respectively, that had sex with men and women in their sleep. They acquired a sinister reputation partly because of religions that consider sex to be sinful, and partly because erotic dreams carried through to completion often resulted in physical tiredness - it wasn't a great leap to then think that sex 'depletes the life-force'. The creatures are usually beautiful and are fully in control in the dream, creating a pleasurably half-fearful, half-lustful feeling in the dreamer.

In your dream: They may represent someone trying to take your lover away from you or your fear of not being attractive enough to hold onto your partner. Alternatively they may reveal a hankering to hand over control to a lover, especially if you're usually the one who has to make all the moves. If neither of these scenarios apply, the dream may be just an erotic fantasy and best enjoyed as such.

Werewolf

While just about any creature could be involved in **metamorphosis**, the wolf is probably the best known, perhaps because of the romance associated with the wolf (see Wolf, page 82). The werewolf is a complex image, part **victim**, part **predator**. It embodies the idea of becoming something more powerful than yourself in order to enact **vengeance** on those who have hurt you – but with no accompanying guilt, as the mind becomes animal, acting on instinct. Guilt comes later as memories of actions taken while in wolf form resurface in the human brain. At its most tragic, the werewolf kills its own loved ones. Yet there's a powerful appeal in the idea of being able to borrow an animal's natural skills and experience its life for a time.

In your dream: Were you a werewolf or did you meet one? What feelings were associated with the dream – do you feel yourself to be a victim in your waking life, or do you fantasize about 'getting your own back' on those who have hurt you, in a form that leaves the human you blameless?

Dwarf

Traditionally, dwarfs are small, secretive, long-lived people who live in caves and under the earth, and are skilled metal-workers and jewellers.

In your dream: What were the dwarfs doing? They may symbolize your own hidden talents, digging the 'gems' of inspiration and imagination from the depths of your mind. Alternatively, were they hiding treasure? Are you afraid of others stealing your ideas?

Ogre

The most notable things about ogres are that they are huge in size and they eat humans.

In your dream: Dreaming of an ogre suggests that you feel someone important or superior in your waking life is 'eating you alive'. Does the dream indicate any way to escape?

Fairy, elf, fey folk

The term 'fey folk' encompasses all human-appearing supernatural beings – fairies and elves, principally. In legends they were attractive, could be kind or malevolent, took offence easily and were seen as being immortal and having magical powers. Fairies are seen as small, winged nature spirits, protective of flowers and plants; elves as beautiful humanoids, shy or aloof. Their symbolism in dreams depends on your personal perception of them.

In your dream: Were they trying to protect something or guide you somewhere? Or were they mischievous, leading you astray? Dreaming of the fey folk suggests that you feel forces entirely outside your control have a grip on your life.

Merfolk

Half fish, half human, merfolk – most often female – have haunted human consciousness for centuries.

In your dream: These usually beautiful creatures may represent the embodiment of your emotions, or they may be a symbol of your anima or animus.
(See Anima/Animus, page 147)

Witch, wizard

Witches and wizards are no longer viewed as dark, evil creatures, but as magic-wielders with the same urges and needs as ordinary folk – which makes for a far more interesting, complex and morally ambiguous world, requiring a more tolerant, reflective frame of mind.

In your dream: Was the magic-user benevolent or malevolent? Were they using their powers to help others or to influence those around them? This figure can represent someone you mistrust or can't understand in your waking life: your subconscious may be warning you to avoid them if possible. Alternatively, the dream may express a wish that you could 'wave a **magic wand**' and make all your troubles vanish without trace!

Monster

Monsters can take any form, but often appear in dreams as a creature composed of all the things we most fear – spidery, snaky things with tentacles, dripping venom, fangs or claws, or something less obvious, shadowy, half-glimpsed and threatening figures that create a sense of doom.

In your dream: Learning to deal with your personal dream monster can be very empowering – the feeling of triumph carries over to your waking life and can help you to cope with daily problems. You need to consider how best to handle the situation. Do you hunt it? Challenge it? Form a set of rules which it has to obey? Having someone else deal with it? Or is talking to it the most appropriate method?

Ghost

Ghosts in dreams are more likely to be images of people or occasionally pets, we have loved and lost through separation or bereavement, than of strangers.

In your dream: Such a dream may be wish-fulfilment or your subconscious providing a measure of closure, especially if the ghost represents someone with whom you have unfinished business. This person may be a parent, sibling or partner who died before you had apologized or explained yourself, or told them how you felt about them – or a lover who left after a row you now regret. A dream of a stranger ghost may symbolize a wish for advice from an outside source. Take note of what the ghost says or does.

Aliens

In dreams, as in films, aliens generally tend to be vaguely humanoid: our imaginations are fuelled by what is portrayed on the screen or in drawings. Aliens are to some extent the modern version of the stranger, something 'not us'. Your response to the strange and unfamiliar in waking life is more than likely your response to the same in dreams, but it may prevent you from learning or taking advantage of opportunities.

In your dream: Did you dream of being abducted? If so, do you feel that you have lost control of your life, that other far more powerful people are treating you as an object or guinea pig? If they were friendly or neutral aliens, did you greet them with enthusiasm, demand to know what they wanted, or run away in fear? What did the aliens do? Offer help and advancement, take offence, leave?
(See also Space, page 36; Spacecraft, page 202)

Demon

Many religions have demons, mischievous or hostile beings intent on causing obstruction or harm to humans. Individuals who 'bedevil' you in waking life may appear in dreams as demons.

In your dream: Your subconscious may be anticipating the actions of someone who is causing you trouble, or could do. Does the dream show any way out of the situation?

Robot

Robots aren't supernatural, of course, but they do possess that same quality of being like us, but utterly unlike us – superficially humanoid but devoid of feelings or non-logical thought. Their appearance in dreams may have connotations of a bright new work-free world or perhaps something more menacing.

In your dream: Do you wish for a mechanical person to take on the burden of all the things you loathe doing or are you afraid that machines will take over, making the human race into their slaves?

Superhero

The heroes of ancient mythology still exist, in the form of the super-powered humanoids, aliens and mutants of popular culture. Dreaming of being a superhero isn't uncommon, especially if you feel misunderstood or alienated from your native society (as many people do).

In your dream: A dream of possessing **special powers** that can be used for good or ill usually symbolizes a yearning to have some control over your life and destiny.

Divination

Images of a **crystal ball, Tarot pack, I Ching** sticks, **runes** or **astrological** symbols suggest you are uncertain about your future and longing to find out what is 'on the cards'. Since time immemorial humans have tried to find ways to predict what will happen, in order to try to avert disaster or take advantage of any opportunities. Dreams themselves have often been used as a form of prediction. It has never been proved that any form of prediction is wholly effective, although it can be argued that chance alone will ensure that occasionally a prediction will come true.

In your dream: Dreaming of consulting a fortune teller of some kind suggests you feel very uncertain about the outcome of a particular project or affair, and need advice that science or a recognized expert might not be able to give you – or is not what you wish to hear. Dreaming of being a diviner of some sort may simply indicate that you would very much like to be 'psychic' in some way, or believe that you already have some psychic ability. If this is the case, consider what form of prediction you were using in the dream and explore it in waking life.

INDEX

ACKNOWLEDGEMENTS

Executive Editor Sandra Rigby
Editors Alice Bowden, Lisa John
Executive Art Editor Sally Bond
Designer Grade Design Consultants, London
Illustrator Andrew Pavitt
Production Manager Louise Hall